LIVING IN HIS

SUFFICIENCY

Based on
Colossians

CHARLES
STANLEY

OLIVER
NELSON

THOMAS NELSON PUBLISHERS
Nashville

CONTENTS

WHERE DO WE GO FOR "WHAT'S MISSING"?

When you experience a crisis in your life, where do you turn *first*?

When you have an unmet need in your life, to whom do you go for immediate assistance?

When you are faced with a difficult question or problem, what is your first source of reference?

When you recognize that "something's missing" in your life—when you have a lack of provision, security, hope, love, safety, comfort, or self-identity—from whom or what do you seek supply?

The answer to these questions for a genuine Christian must be a resounding, "Christ Jesus!" To turn to any person, group, organization, or entity *other than* Christ Jesus for one's total provision and supply in life—both external and internal—is to deny, to some degree, the sufficiency of Christ.

In the first century, false teachers made claims to the new believers that Jesus Christ might be sufficient for some of their needs—perhaps even many or most of their needs—but that other traditional customs and beliefs were necessary *in addition to Christ* for a person to experience a total supply of all things. They taught that while Christ Jesus might be sufficient for a person's spiritual salvation, Christ Jesus could not fulfill all practical, emotional, material, or social needs.

The apostle Paul soundly rejected the claims of these false teachers in a letter that we know as the book of Colossians in the New Testament. This entire letter is devoted to Paul's claim that Christ Jesus is 100 percent *sufficient* to meet all human needs, now and forever.

"But what," you may ask, "does this have to do with me today? Paul was writing to people who lived in the ancient past, not the modern world."

The same arguments that were made to the believers in the early church are being made to Christians and non-Christians today! The sufficiency of Christ Jesus is attacked from many sides, at times directly and boldly, and at times indirectly and with great subtlety.

Some will say . . .

"Jesus was a good man who lived and taught two thousand years ago . . . but you need more than the teachings of Jesus to live a victorious and prosperous life in the world today."

"Believing in Jesus is good, but if you really want to have spiritual experiences that will make you feel good, you also should try . . ."

"Christ Jesus is sufficient for your salvation . . . but you also need to do X, Y, and Z to *ensure* your place in heaven."

"A faith in Christ is great for your spiritual life, but you need to hear the teachings of Mr. A and Ms. B and Preacher C if you are going to enjoy inner growth and material prosperity."

"No," says Paul to the Colossians and to us, "you don't need anything beyond Christ Jesus."

In my work as a pastor I have encountered countless church-going, Christ-believing people who have fallen prey to arguments that Christ is not sufficient to meet all of their needs. The main reason seems to be this: They do *not fully* know Christ Jesus. Very specifically:

- They do not know the fullness of His deity.
- They do not have an intimate and ongoing, daily relationship with Him, which means that they do not truly *know* Him, they only know *about* Him.

This Bible study explores the sufficiency of Christ. It is focused primarily on the book of Colossians, although many other Bible references are included. It deals with three questions that are vital to the life of every believer:

1. Who is Christ Jesus—*really?*
2. What has Christ Jesus already provided for me as a person who believes that He is the Son of God?
3. How can I experience the full sufficiency of Christ Jesus in my life on a practical and personal level?

The fact is, if we don't fully know Christ Jesus, we cannot know His sufficiency. And if we do not believe that He is sufficient, and have an ability to access His sufficiency, we are vulnerable to arguments that can lead us astray—away from Christ and away from the perfection to which Christ calls us.

On the other hand, if we have a deep understanding of all that Christ has provided for us and all that He makes available to us, we have a solid foundation on which to grow and develop *in every area of our lives.* A solid foundation, one established on the eternal principles of God's Word, must become our desire if we truly are to live meaningful, satisfying, and victorious lives!

OUR SUFFICIENCY, SOURCE, AND SUPPLY

*S*ufficiency—*all* that is needed in ample supply.

Supply—what is needed to meet a particular need, solve a particular problem, or overcome a particular lack.

Source—a fountainhead of supply that produces sufficiency.

These three terms—*sufficiency, supply, and source*—will be used almost interchangeably in this book because Jesus Christ *is* our Sufficiency for an abundant life, our Supply or Provision, and our Source of wholeness in this life and eternal life in the future.

How do we know this? Because that is what the Bible teaches about Jesus Christ.

This book is intended for Bible study, and the lessons in it are based upon the belief that the Bible gives us the whole truth and nothing but the truth about Jesus Christ. My hope as you engage in this study is that you will turn again and again to your favorite version of the Bible to highlight specific words, underline phrases, write in the margins, or circle verses that speak to you in a special way. Make this study *your* study about the sufficiency of Christ and feel free to mark dates, notes, and insights into your personal Bible.

Countless other books tell about methods and means other than Christ as a foundation for wholeness, sufficiency, and everlasting supply. The Bible, however, is God's truth about who Jesus Christ is—*really*—and about what Christ provides for us. It is when we understand and apply what the Bible says that we truly come to *know* Christ Jesus as our Sufficiency. Make the Bible your ultimate authority on Jesus Christ and how to get your needs met, and you won't be disappointed!

For Personal or Group Study

You may use this guide on your own or as part of a small-group study. If you use this book for individual Bible study, you will find many places in which to note your response to the material presented or to record your insights. If you are using this book for small-group study, you'll find questions to trigger discussion.

At various times, you will be asked to identify with the material in one of these ways:

- What new insight have you gained?
- Have you ever had a similar experience?
- How do you feel about the material?
- In what way do you feel challenged to action?

Insights

To see something in the Scriptures "as if for the first time" is to have an insight. An insight is more than a mere fact or idea—it is related to *meaning.* When you see a deeper meaning or discover a way in which a truth of God's Word might be applied to your own life, that is a spiritual insight.

Most of us have had the experience of reading a passage of the Bible countless times and then one day upon reading it exclaim, "I never saw that before!" When that happens, you are experiencing an insight.

Insights are usually very personal. They often occur because what we read stands out to us with respect to something we are currently experiencing or have recently experienced. At other times, they help us pull together information or meaning in a new way that is helpful to us in resolving a problem or making a decision. An insight can result in a sudden "knowing" about what to do, how to think, what to say, or why we believe what we believe.

Ask God to give you insights every time you open His Word to read it. I believe He will answer that prayer! And, as you have insights, make notes about them. If you are intentional about recording your insights, you will likely find that you are having more and more insights. The more you actively listen for God to speak to you, the more He does! If you haven't gained new spiritual insights after reading several passages from God's Word, you probably haven't been engaged in the process of study, or you may have let your mind wander as you were reading. Ask as you read, "What is God saying to *me*? How might this apply to my life?"

From time to time in this guide, you will be asked to note what a specific passage of the Bible is saying to you. Make sure that your response is a personal response, not simply a recording of what you perceive to be the group's response.

Experiences

We each come to God's Word from a unique background and with a built-in set of experiences that relate to the sufficiency of Christ. We each have a unique perspective, therefore, on what we believe about Jesus Christ and how we approach God's Word.

Rather than focus on your *opinions* about Christ, however, this study asks that you point to *life experiences* you have had with Christ Jesus and with the application of God's Word. We each have had experiences about which we can say, "I know that truth in the Bible is valid because of what happened to me." We have had experiences with God's Word that challenged us, convicted us, and at times encouraged or comforted us.

Now, our experiences do not make the Bible true. The Bible is truth. But there is great value in our sharing experiences because they help us to see the many ways in which the Bible is applicable to us and to others. We see how God's Word has the potential to speak to every person and to address at some level every circumstance or situation a person might encounter. The more we share experiences with one another, the more we discover that God's Word is universal—it applies to all people at all times—as well as highly personal and individual.

Sharing experiences is important for spiritual growth. If you are doing this study on your own, I encourage you to talk to others about what you are reading in God's Word, what it means to you, and ways in which God's Word has had bearing on your life.

Emotional Responses

Just as we each have unique experiences, we also have highly individualized emotional responses to what we read in God's Word. Face your emotions honestly and learn to share them with others. Don't be ashamed of having an emotional response to God's Word. God expects you to respond to Him and to His Word in an emotional way—He gave you your emotions and He intends for you to learn how to use your emotions in a healthful and beneficial way.

At times, you may feel uneasy or fearful about something you read in God's Word. At other times, you may feel restless because you have questions. At still other times, you may feel very comforted, assured, and loved in response to what you read. As you identify your emotions toward God's truth, you are in a very good position to ask, "*Why* am I feeling this way?" Very likely, the Lord is speaking to you in a personal way that can lead to your spiritual growth and to a greater intimacy in your relationship with Him.

In virtually all cases in a small group, it is more helpful for people to express their emotional responses than to give their opinions. Strong personal opinions tend to divide groups. Sharing emotional responses tends to build empathy and to unite groups spiritually.

The more you study about Christ's sufficiency, the stronger your emotional response toward Jesus Christ is likely to be. My prayer is that you will feel a great surge of joy, confidence, and deep, abiding inner peace as you complete this study.

Challenges

God's Word inevitably challenges or convicts us at some point. God is never satisfied with our status quo. No matter how mature we may be as Christians, there is always some way in which we can be conformed more closely to the likeness of Christ Jesus. Allow God's Word to speak to *you*.

God's Word may bring about a conviction of sin. Or, it may be a clear call to engage in a new behavior or to pursue a new avenue of ministry or service. At times, a closer reading of God's Word may significantly alter our own understanding of God's love, provision, and sufficiency for our lives. God's Word *always* is aimed at building up our faith, and making our faith active, energized, alive, and applicable. Look for the specific ways in which God's Word motivates you toward taking action.

God desires to get His Word into us so that we might take His Word into the world—to live it out and to be witnesses of His Word in all we say and do. It isn't enough for us to note our insights, recall our experiences, or share our emotions. We must apply what we learn. The Bible challenges us to be doers of His Word and not hearers only (James 1:22).

It isn't enough, in other words, for you to recognize and claim the sufficiency of Christ solely for your own life. You must seek ways in which you can share this good news! God is calling you to be an advocate for Christ's sufficiency to others in your family, your church, and your circle of friends and acquaintances.

Keep the Bible Central

Keep the Bible central to your study. Otherwise you face the danger of your group becoming a therapy or support group, or of it becoming a discussion forum for doctrinal or theological points of view. Refer again and again to the Scriptures. Take what the Bible says at face value—God means what God says! I have discovered that most people understand the vast majority of what they read in the Bible—if they only will make the effort to read it! The trouble is not that we can't understand God's Word; the problem is that we don't read and study it. If at any time, however, you do not understand what the Bible is saying, ask the Holy Spirit to reveal to you the understanding that you need—either individually or as a group. I believe He will be faithful in answering your genuine heart's cry. God's desire is not that we reach group consensus about Jesus Christ, but rather, that our opinions line up with what God says in His Word about Jesus Christ.

If you are doing a personal Bible study, you also must be diligent in staying focused on God's Word. Growing into the fullness of the stature of Christ Jesus is the goal!

Prayer

I encourage you to begin and end your Bible study sessions in prayer. Ask God to give you spiritual ears to hear what He wants you to hear and spiritual eyes to see what He wants you to see. Ask Him to give you new insights, to recall to your memory the experiences that are helpful to your growth and to the growth of others in your group, and to help you identify your emotional responses with clarity. Be bold in asking God to reveal to you what He desires for you to do next in your spiritual journey as you apply the truth of the Bible.

As you conclude your time of study, ask the Lord to seal to your heart what you have learned so that you will not forget it. Ask Him to transform you more into the likeness of Christ Jesus as you meditate on what you have studied. Ask Him to do a work in you that is lasting and has eternal benefits.

The Depths of God's Word

Avoid the temptation of concluding at the end of your ten-lesson study that you know all there is to know about the sufficiency of Christ. To know *and experience* the sufficiency of Christ is an *everlasting* pursuit because to know Christ is to have an eternal relationship with Christ. Can you ever know a dearly beloved spouse or friend well enough? No! The same is true for Christ Jesus. There's always something more about Christ that He longs to reveal to you.

Never stop exploring the riches of God's Word on any topic, but especially on the sufficiency of Christ Jesus. The truth of Christ's sufficiency is a lesson that is always timely, and that is always applicable in new ways. Grow in your understanding . . . and choose to continue growing in your understanding of His sufficiency all the days of your life.

- *What questions do you presently have about the sufficiency of Christ? Are there areas of your life in which you doubt that He is sufficient? Acknowledge those. They are likely to be the areas in which you will have the most spiritual insights.*

- *Have you had experiences in which you knew with certainty that Christ was sufficient to meet all your needs?*

- *What is your emotional response to the statement, "Christ Jesus is sufficient for all things"?*

  _____

  _____

- *What do you hope to gain from a study of Christ's sufficiency?*

  _____

  _____

WHO IS JESUS . . . REALLY?

Jesus made a tremendous claim about Himself in John 14:6 when He said: "I am the way, the truth, and the life. No one comes to the Father except through Me."

Who is the One who makes such a claim about Himself? How does this claim impact a person's faith? If a person truly believes this claim made by Jesus, how does his belief change the way he lives? These are important questions for every Christian to answer.

Countless people in our world refute this claim made by Jesus, saying, "There are many paths to God. There are many religions, but as long as they all point in the same direction, they are to a great extent equal." Others are indignant at His claim, saying in effect, "How dare He think He is the only way to the Father." Still others try to discredit the claim of Jesus, saying that He didn't really *mean* what is written or that He didn't really *say* what John wrote. Genuine Christian believers through the ages, however, have staked their lives on this claim that Jesus made about Himself.

Our belief about Jesus Christ determines several important aspects of our faith:

- The relationship we believe we have with God

- How we respond to Jesus Christ
- How we live our lives in relationship to other people
- The power of our faith

  - *How do you respond to what Jesus said about Himself? What emotions does His statement cause you to feel?*

_____

_____

  - *In what ways are you challenged by this claim of Jesus?*

_____

_____

Not a New Argument

The apostle Paul wrote the book of Colossians to counter the arguments that were being circulated by a number of false teachers who claimed that Jesus was a good man but that belief in Him was not required or sufficient for salvation. These were teachers who advocated that other doctrines and cults had their place as equals to Christianity.

In response to these false teachers, Paul said, "Don't let anyone delude you. Don't be misled!" As you read the several verses of warning from Paul below, consider what it means to be deceived or "cheated" by those who give false instruction.

What the Word Says	What the Word Says to Me
Now this I say lest anyone should deceive you with persuasive words. For though I am absent in the flesh, yet I am with you in spirit, rejoicing to see your good order and the steadfastness of your faith in Christ. (Col. 2:4–5)	_____ _____ _____ _____ _____ _____ _____

Beware lest anyone cheat you
through philosophy and empty
deceit, according to the tradition of men, according to the
basic principles of the world,
and not according to Christ.
(Col. 2:8)

_____
_____
_____
_____
_____
_____
_____

- *Have you had an experience in your life when you felt you were misled by "persuasive words," by the "traditions of men," or by the "principles of the world"?*

  _____

  _____

- *How did you feel when you became aware that you had been taught something that was NOT truth according to the Bible?*

  _____

  _____

Paul further responded to these false teachers by presenting two main arguments, both of which will be examined in closer detail in the first two lessons of this book:

1. The false teachers have a wrong understanding about the deity of Jesus Christ. They do not understand that He truly was God incarnate, or God "in flesh."
2. The false teachers have a wrong understanding about the blood of Jesus Christ and what His death on the cross really meant. They do not understand the atonement that was made by Jesus Christ for the sins of all mankind.

Certainly it is not fully possible for any of us, in our finite human state, to comprehend the *fullness* of our infinite God. None of us are fully capable of comprehending the glory of the Trinity or the majesty of Jesus Christ. To a certain extent, all that we know about God the Father, Jesus Christ, and the Holy Spirit are things that we know *in part*. As Paul wrote to the Corinthians, "Now I know in part, but then I shall know just as I also am known" (1 Cor. 13:12).

Even so, there are some truths that we can know with certainty about God because Jesus Christ made those things very plain to us and explained them not only in words, but by the actions of His life. Paul made a concise and powerful statement about Jesus Christ in the opening verses of his letter to the Colossians. This statement summarizes Paul's teaching about *who* Jesus really was and is. These are facts about God that Paul knew with certainty:

> He is the image of the invisible God, the firstborn over all creation. For by Him all things were created that are in heaven and that are on earth, visible and invisible, whether thrones or dominions or principalities or powers. All things were created through Him and for Him. And He is before all things, and in Him all things consist. And He is the head of the body, the church, who is the beginning, the firstborn from the dead, that in all things He may have the preeminence.
>
> For it pleased the Father that in Him all the fullness should dwell, and by Him to reconcile all things to Himself, by Him, whether things on earth or things in heaven, having made peace through the blood of His cross. (Col. 1:15–20)

• *What insights do you have into this passage of Scripture?*

_____

_____

The Image of the Invisible God

Paul makes as his first statement about Jesus Christ that He is "the image of the invisible God" (Col. 1:15). The

Hebrew people had long held to the belief that God was Spirit—invisible to man and clothed in brilliant light. Just as a person cannot look directly into the sun at high noon, so a person is incapable of looking fully and directly at the glory of God.

What the Word Says	What the Word Says to Me
No one has seen God at any time. The only begotten Son, who is in the bosom of the Father, He has declared Him. (John 1:18)	
I urge you in the sight of God who gives life to all things, and before Christ Jesus . . . He who is the blessed and only Potentate, the King of kings and Lord of lords, who alone has immortality, dwelling in unapproachable light, whom no man has seen or can see, to whom be honor and everlasting power. (1 Tim. 6:13, 15–16)	
O LORD my God, You are very great: You are clothed with honor and majesty, Who cover Yourself with light as with a garment, Who stretch out the heavens like a curtain. (Ps. 104:1–2)	

The Jews also believed, however, that God manifested Himself in humanlike form from time to time for the purposes of communicating eternal truth to mankind or to give certain prophets very specific direction or assistance. There are a number of instances in the Old Testament of "the Lord" having physical characteristics—a form that many Bible scholars term "the pre-incarnate Christ." For example, Jacob wrestled with Him; and Shadrach, Meshach, and Abed-Nego, three Hebrew captives in Babylon, walked with Him in a burning furnace. God "put on" a fleshlike appearance, but God the Father is *not* flesh.

What the Word Says	What the Word Says to Me
Then Jacob was left alone; and a Man wrestled with him until the breaking of day . . . Then Jacob asked, saying, "Tell me Your name, I pray." . . . And He blessed him there. So Jacob called the name of the place Peniel: "For I have seen God face to face, and my life is preserved." (Gen. 32:24, 29–30)	----------------------------
"Look!" he [Nebuchadnezzar] answered, "I see four men loose, walking in the midst of the fire; and they are not hurt, and the form of the fourth is like the Son of God." (Dan. 3:25)	----------------------------

Who is Jesus? Jesus is the *incarnate* Son of God. He walked on this earth as God fully clothed in flesh, not appearing for a very brief period as with the patriarchs or prophets of old, but manifesting Himself to all who would believe in Him and follow Him. He was "God made man."

If you truly grasp this truth of God's Word, you can never think of Jesus again as "just a good man." Jesus *was* and *is* God in fleshly form.

What the Word Says

In the beginning was the Word,
and the Word was with God,
and the Word was God . . .
And the Word became flesh
and dwelt among us, and we
beheld His glory, the glory as
of the only begotten of the
Father, full of grace and truth.
(John 1:1, 14)

Jesus said to him [Philip],
"Have I been with you so long,
and yet you have not known
Me, Philip? He who has seen
Me has seen the Father; so
how can you say, 'Show us the
Father'? Do you not believe
that I am in the Father, and
the Father in Me? The words
that I speak to you I do not
speak on My own authority;
but the Father who dwells in
Me does the works." (John
14:9–10)

[Jesus said,] "Most assuredly, I
say to you, the Son can do
nothing of Himself, but what

What the Word Says to Me

He sees the Father do; for whatever He does, the Son also does in like manner. For the Father loves the Son, and shows Him all things that He Himself does; and He will show Him greater works than these, that you may marvel . . . He who does not honor the Son does not honor the Father who sent Him. (John 5:19–20, 23)

[Jesus said,] "I and My Father are one." (John 10:30)

[Jesus said,] "Believe the works, that you may know and believe that the Father is in Me, and I in Him." (John 10:38)

[Jesus said,] "All things that I heard from My Father I have made known to you." (John 15:15)

[Jesus said,] "All things that the Father has are Mine. Therefore I said that He will take of Mine and declare it to you." (John 16:15)

[Jesus prayed,] "Father . . . You loved Me before the foundation of the world. O righteous

Father! The world has not
known You, but I have known
You; and these have known
that You sent Me. And I have
declared to them Your name,
and will declare it, that the
love with which You loved Me
may be in them, and I in
them." (John 17:24–26)

Jesus was not just a godly man. He was "God made man."
All others who have claimed to be a "god" have been blemished, flawed, or tainted by sin in some way . . . but not Jesus.
He was perfect, without sin. He was the "only begotten Son" of
God (John 3:16).

What the Word Says	What the Word Says to Me
Who committed no sin, Nor was deceit found in His mouth. (1 Peter 2:22)	------------------------------ ------------------------------ ------------------------------
You were not redeemed with corruptible things . . . but with the precious blood of Christ, as of a lamb without blemish and without spot. (1 Peter 1:18–19)	------------------------------ ------------------------------ ------------------------------ ------------------------------ ------------------------------

Paul stated very plainly that Jesus was the "fullness" of
God—a full manifestation of God's character and nature. In
other words, there was nothing about God's nature that was
not manifested in Jesus Christ, and there was nothing in Jesus
Christ that was not a perfect match of the Father's nature. Paul
wrote:

> For it pleased the Father that in Him [Jesus Christ] all
> the fullness should dwell, and by Him to reconcile all
> things to Himself. (Col. 1:19–20)

> For in Him dwells all the fullness of the Godhead bodily. (Col. 2:9)

In His flesh, Jesus was fully man. In His Spirit—His nature,
His character, His inner being—He was fully God. He was
God clothed in human flesh, walking on this earth and showing us *by His life*—His words and deeds—the nature and will
of God the Father.

Let this truth sink deep into your spirit! Jesus was and is
God the Son.

- *What new insights do you have into the identity of Jesus Christ?*

_____

_____

- *How do you feel about Jesus being God the Son?*

_____

_____

Why Did God Reveal Himself as Jesus?

Why did Jesus come to this earth? What was the purpose of
God revealing Himself in this way? One of the foremost reasons was so that we might truly *know* God. God desired for
mankind to know Him in a more intimate way—to know His
heartbeat, mind, plans and purposes, nature and character.
Read what the writer to the Hebrews said:

> God, who at various times and in various ways spoke in
> time past to the fathers by the prophets, has in these last
> days spoken to us by His Son, whom He has appointed

heir of all things, through whom also He made the worlds; who being the brightness of His glory and the express image of His person, and upholding all things by the word of His power. (1:1–3)

Jesus came to show us what God is like. He came to *explain* God to us. He came as the "express image" of God to speak to us God's words and to show us how God thinks, feels, and loves.

So many people today say they know God but they don't want anything to do with Jesus. That simply is not possible! Jesus was and is God. God cannot be known directly apart from Jesus.

Ask yourself, "What is it that I truly know about God *apart* from Christ Jesus?" The answer is, "Nothing!" If a person looks at this world to know God apart from Christ, he is left with natural laws alone—and friend, nature does not give us a full or accurate picture of God because we live in a fallen world that has been greatly impacted by man's sinful nature. How can a person know about the love of God, the mercy of God, the joy of knowing God apart from Christ Jesus? It isn't possible. Jesus came to *show* us the Father in a way that we could fully understand. As a child once said, "Jesus is God with a face and arms."

What the Word Says	What the Word Says to Me
For it is the God who commanded light to shine out of darkness, who has shone in our hearts to give the light of the knowledge of the glory of God in the face of Jesus Christ. (2 Cor. 4:6)	_____ _____ _____ _____ _____ _____ _____
[Paul wrote,] To me, who am less than the least of all the	_____ _____

saints, this grace was given,
that I should preach among
the Gentiles the unsearchable
riches of Christ, and to make
all see what is the fellowship of
the mystery, which from the
beginning of the ages has been
hidden in God who created all
things through Jesus Christ; to
the intent that now the mani-
fold wisdom of God might be
made known . . . according to
the eternal purpose which He
accomplished in Christ Jesus
our Lord. (Eph. 3:8–11)

Jesus came to take away the veil of mystery from God's plan and purpose for mankind. He came to make God approachable and understandable to the human heart and mind.

What does this have to do with Christ being our sufficiency? Everything! If Jesus was *not* the Son of God . . . if He was not God . . . if He was not deity . . . then He is not sufficient. But because Jesus is, indeed, God the Son, He is completely sufficient—for what need could we possibly have that God cannot meet, what lack could we possibly experience that God cannot fill, what problem could we possibly have that God cannot solve? God, who is all-powerful, all-wise, all-loving, and who is everpresent and eternal—God who knows the beginning from the ending and who controls and governs all things—is entirely sufficient. And Jesus *is* God.

- *What new insight do you have into the nature and character of Christ Jesus?*

- *In what ways are you feeling challenged in your spirit?*

  _____

  _____

ALL WE NEED FOR RECONCILIATION WITH GOD

Jesus not only came to *show* us what God the Father is like, but to *reconcile* us to God the Father. He accomplished this through His death on the cross, making it possible for all who believe in Christ Jesus to be saved from eternal death. To become reconciled to God we need *only* believe in Jesus Christ as our Savior and to accept what He did on the cross as being on our behalf. Jesus Christ is totally sufficient for our salvation.

There are those in various religions and even Christian denominations who claim that for a person to be fully reconciled to God, he must complete various rituals or fulfill certain types of works or obligations.

God's Word proclaims strongly that no amount of works, effort, or goodness on our part can bring about our salvation. In fact, no one and no thing *other than* Jesus Christ is the Savior. And furthermore, Jesus Christ is fully sufficient to be the Savior—nothing "in addition" to believing in Christ Jesus is necessary for a person to be born again spiritually, to receive God's forgiveness, and to experience the presence of the Holy Spirit.

What the Word Says	What the Word Says to Me
In Him we have redemption through His blood, the forgiveness of sins, according to the riches of His grace which He made to abound toward us. (Eph. 1:7–8)	------------------------------ ------------------------------ ------------------------------ ------------------------------ ------------------------------ ------------------------------
[Jesus said,] And as Moses lifted up the serpent in the wilderness, even so must the Son of Man be lifted up [on the cross], that whoever believes in Him should not perish but have eternal life. (John 3:14–15)	------------------------------ ------------------------------ ------------------------------ ------------------------------ ------------------------------ ------------------------------ ------------------------------ ------------------------------
[Jesus said,] For God so loved the world that He gave His only begotten Son, that whoever believes in Him should not perish but have everlasting life. (John 3:16)	------------------------------ ------------------------------ ------------------------------ ------------------------------ ------------------------------ ------------------------------
For by grace you have been saved through faith, and that not of yourselves; it is the gift of God, not of works, lest anyone should boast. (Eph. 2:8–9)	------------------------------ ------------------------------ ------------------------------ ------------------------------ ------------------------------ ------------------------------
For in Christ Jesus neither circumcision nor uncircumcision avails anything, but a new creation. (Gal. 6:15)	------------------------------ ------------------------------ ------------------------------ ------------------------------

- *What new insights do you have into the sufficiency of Christ for your salvation?*

_____

_____

A Full and Complete Reconciliation

What does it mean to be reconciled to someone, and in particular, to God?

First, the word *reconciliation* implies that a relationship has been "broken" and that it is in need of mending. We each are born into a state of estrangement or "distance" from God.

Now with certainty, God loves us, He created us for Himself, and He desires to be reconciled with us—and this is true every second of our lives. But we each are born with the sin nature that is the inheritance of all human beings after the fall of Adam and Eve. This sin nature separates us from God since God can have no association with sin. We also are given a free will by God from our birth so that we can choose to retain our old sin nature or to turn to God, receive His forgiveness, and receive a "new nature," one that is not rooted in sin.

When Jesus died on the cross as our eternal, definitive, substitutionary sacrifice for sin, He made it possible for those who *accept* what Jesus did to have their sin nature changed and thus, be made *acceptable* for close intimacy with God the Father. Our part in bringing about reconciliation is to say to God the Father, "I believe in Jesus Christ as my Savior. I accept what He did on the cross as being for *my* sins. Please forgive me. Please change my sin nature. Please fill me with Your Holy Spirit so that I can live my life in a way that is totally pleasing to You."

Have you accepted the reconciliation that Jesus Christ makes possible? If not, I encourage you to do so today.

• *In what ways are you feeling challenged in your spirit?*

_____

_____

Reconciliation Brings Change

Believing in Jesus Christ brings about a "newness" in a person. The old sin nature is no more. A new nature that desires the goodness and righteousness of God takes its place. We are no longer the spiritual sons and daughters of Adam and Eve, but we are the spiritual sons and daughters of God the Father.

This change is *not* something that we are required to "work up" on our own. It is not something we must strive to do. Rather, it is the work of Jesus Christ in our lives. He is the One who changes us, from the inside out.

What the Word Says	What the Word Says to Me
But as many as received Him, to them He gave the right to become children of God, to those who believe in His name: who were born, not of blood, nor of the will of the flesh, nor of the will of man, but of God. (John 1:12–13)	_____ _____ _____ _____ _____ _____ _____ _____
Therefore, if anyone is in Christ, he is a new creation; old things have passed away; behold, all things have become new. Now all things are of God, who has reconciled us to Himself through Jesus Christ, and has given us the ministry	_____ _____ _____ _____ _____ _____ _____

of reconciliation, that is, that
God was in Christ reconciling
the world to Himself, not
imputing their trespasses to
them, and has committed to us
the word of reconciliation . . .
For He made Him who knew
no sin to be sin for us, that we
might become the righteousness of God in Him. (2 Cor.
5:17–19, 21)

Paul wrote very specifically about reconciliation and newness of spiritual life to the Colossians:

> For it pleased the Father that in Him all the fullness
> should dwell, and by Him to reconcile all things to
> Himself, by Him, whether things on earth or things in
> heaven, having made peace through the blood of His
> cross. And you, who once were alienated and enemies
> in your mind by wicked works, yet now He has recon-
> ciled in the body of His flesh through death, to present
> you holy, and blameless, and above reproach in His
> sight. (1:19–22)

I want to call your attention to four words and phrases in
this passage from Colossians:

1. Peace. So many people believe that God is in some kind
of cosmic tug-of-war with mankind. God wants one thing, men
and women want another, and God is acting as a harsh judge
to whip mankind into shape. When you read the Bible closely,
however, you will discover a wonderful truth: Jesus came to
war against the devil and against evil, but He came to bring
peace to the hearts of all who would believe in Him.

Jesus came to bring us to a state of deep and abiding "peace"
with God—not just a truce, but a lasting "rest" in our rela-

tionship so that we are no longer at odds with God. When we accept Jesus as Savior and receive His Holy Spirit into our lives, we are made one with Christ and therefore, we are one with the Father. We begin to want what God wants and to desire what God desires.

So many people are looking in all the wrong places to find peace of heart and mind. They think they will find peace of heart by possessing certain things, reaching certain levels of achievement, taking certain chemicals into their bodies, or by entering into certain relationships. Genuine peace is to be found in only one place—in relationship with Jesus Christ. He is completely sufficient for our peace.

- *In your life, what are some of the things you have done to find peace of heart . . . things that failed to give lasting peace?*

_____

_____

- *In your life, have you experienced genuine "peace" with God?*

_____

_____

What the Word Says

[Jesus said,] "These things I have spoken to you, that in Me you may have peace. In the world you will have tribulation; but be of good cheer, I have overcome the world." (John 16:33)

[Jesus prayed,] "I do not pray for these alone, but also for

What the Word Says to Me

_____

_____

_____

_____

_____

_____

_____

_____

those who will believe in Me
through their word; that they
all may be one, as You, Father,
are in Me, and I in You; that
they also may be one in Us."
(John 17:20–21)

----

2. Holy. The word *holy* means "separate." Those who are indwelled by Jesus Christ are separate from those who do not believe in Jesus as Savior and Lord of their lives. When you accept Jesus and are born again, God no longer sees you as part of the teeming mass of sinful humanity but as His own child. He looks upon you the same way He looks upon Christ who dwells in you: You are His beloved son or daughter.

3. Blameless. To be blameless means that there are no eternal consequences associated with your old sin nature. In God's eyes, your salvation completely frees you from the eternal consequences of sin. God no longer even remembers your sin once you accept His forgiveness. What freedom that brings to the person who fully grasps this truth!

4. Above reproach. To be above reproach means that God has no reservations whatsoever about associating with you. He longs to be with you, to spend time with you, to communicate with you, and to shower upon you His unending love. He desires an intimate, daily, walking-and-talking relationship with you.

• *How do you feel about being called holy, blameless, and above reproach before God?*

What the Word Says

What the Word Says to Me

Just as He chose us in Him
before the foundation of the
world, that we should be holy

----

and without blame before Him
in love. (Eph. 1:4)

God, who has saved us and
called us with a holy calling,
not according to our works,
but according to His own purpose and grace which was
given to us in Christ Jesus
before time began. (2 Tim.
1:8–9)

What a glorious identity we have with God the Father once we have accepted Jesus Christ as our Savior and have been reconciled to God through His shed blood!

"But what," you may ask, "does this mean to me in my everyday life?" It means a great deal.

It means that you no longer need to strive to get good enough for good. So many people today are trying to earn enough "points" to gain God's favor or to secure a home in heaven. So many people are striving to do good works in hopes that they will win God's love. God's Word says that all you need to do to be fully reconciled to God is to believe in Jesus Christ!

It also means that you no longer need to be concerned about your own reputation or success. Now, I don't mean that a person needs to stop working, planning, witnessing for Christ, or participating in worthwhile ministry activities. Rather, I mean that a person no longer needs to feel that he is totally responsible for the *effectiveness* of what he does. God calls us to be faithful, and as we are faithful, He brings about the results of our faithfulness in His time, according to His methods, and always for His eternal purposes.

The Lord may call you to preach or teach . . . but He is the One who converts the hearts of men and women.

The Lord may call you to pray for those in need . . . but He is the One who heals and makes whole.

The Lord may call you to give generously to the work of His kingdom . . . but He is the One who multiplies the gifts that are given and rewards those who give in ways that are beyond any taint of manipulation or calculation.

Your reputation and standing before God are secured 100 percent by Jesus Christ. He is your Savior. He is your identity before the Father. He is the One who is at work within you to do *His* good pleasure.

- *As you reflect back on your life, can you identify a time when you were striving to "get good enough" for God?*

_____

_____

- *As you reflect back on your life, can you identify a time or experience in which you felt you had to "improve your reputation" or standing before God?*

_____

_____

- *How do you feel about Christ Jesus being all that you need for full reconciliation and relationship with God the Father?*

_____

_____

- *In what ways are you feeling challenged in your spirit today?*

_____

_____

ALL WE NEED TO FEEL CONFIDENT AND BE EFFECTIVE

Many people say that they would like to "feel confident" in a given situation or more confident in general. What is to be the basis for our confidence as Christians?

Too often we look at particular outward manifestations and traits as signs of confidence. For example, we tend to feel more confident if we are dressed well, know that we look acceptable, are with the "right" people, or feel that we have sufficient courage, information, or skill to face a given task.

Real confidence, however, arises from who we are on the "inside." Confidence can be broken down into several traits:

- Having the power to be effective or to make a difference
- Having the resources necessary to be effective
- Having the insight, wisdom, or information necessary to make choices and decisions that truly matter and that make a difference in the lives of others, as well as ourselves

- Having the inner fortitude to endure criticism or ridicule and emerge on the side of right
- Having the "status" necessary to get a job done
- Having a reputation of past achievement
- Feeling a special calling of God to undertake a specific task, knowing by faith that we will succeed

Who is it that gives us such confidence?

Christ Jesus! Ultimately, Christ Jesus is the only One who *can* give us genuine confidence, and who can make us effective in all that He leads us to undertake. As Christians, who we are on the inside relates directly to whom we have dwelling in us—Christ Jesus!

This is not to discount the contribution of unconditional love from parents, teachers, and others in the lives of a child, or the unconditional love received from others as an adult. Jesus Christ, however, is the only One who can *fully* satisfy our needs for love, acceptance, belonging, competency, and worthiness.

The Source of Our Confidence

In Revelation 5:12 we find the angels and elders of heaven saying with a loud voice around the throne of God:

Worthy is the Lamb who was slain
To receive power and riches and wisdom,
And strength and honor and glory and blessing!

Every creature in heaven, on earth, and in the sea then joins this throng of angels and elders in saying,

Blessing and honor and glory and power
Be to Him who sits on the throne,
And to the Lamb, forever and ever. (Rev. 5:13)

Jesus alone is worthy. He is the One from whom all power,

riches, wisdom, strength, honor, glory, and blessing come! In other words, He is the One who imparts to us the power or strength that we may be lacking but are required for us to be effective and to make a difference for good. He is the One who imparts to us the resources, wisdom, enduring strength, status, reputation, and faith-calling that we need to be effective. All of the traits we desire as a part of "self-confidence" are resident in Jesus Christ and they are imparted from Him to us.

- *How has Christ Jesus met the need for various aspects of confidence in your life?*

  _____

  _____

- *In your life, have you experienced times when you relied on someone or something other than Jesus Christ as the foundation for your confidence? What was the result?*

  _____

  _____

We can base 100 percent of our confidence on Christ for three reasons:

1. Jesus Christ alone knows who we are . . . completely.
2. Jesus Christ alone knows what is missing in our lives.
3. Jesus Christ alone can *supply* to us what is missing to make us whole and to make us effective.

Jesus Christ Knows Us Completely

Jesus Christ knows us completely because He was with the Father when we were made. He knows exactly who we are, and what we are capable of being and doing, because He was present at our creation.

Paul wrote to the Colossians that Jesus was "the firstborn over all creation" (1:15). He also wrote,

> For by Him all things were created that are in heaven and that are on earth, visible and invisible, whether thrones or dominions or principalities or powers. All things were created through Him and for Him. And He is before all things, and in Him all things consist." (1:16–17)

What does it mean for Jesus to be the "firstborn"? "First," in this case, refers to position, preeminence, and power, not first in time or chronology. He is the firstborn "over" all creation, not the firstborn "of" creation. We refer to the wife of the President of the United States as the First Lady. This does not mean that she was the first president's wife, or the first woman ever to fill this position. It means she is considered to be in an elevated position of prestige. Jesus is the *first*, the preeminent, the most important, the most prestigious, the most revered, the most worthy.

Our Author and Finisher

Paul says that all things were created by Jesus Christ "through Him and for Him" (v. 16).

Jesus Christ is your "author." He knows the full story of your life, with all the details. He is also your "finisher"—He is the One who can impart to you the power and ability to bring your story to its full completion (Heb. 12:2).

What does it mean to you and me to know that Jesus was present at our creation and that He knows *every* detail of our lives from start to finish? It means that nothing about us is a secret or a surprise to Jesus. He knows our present capacity, our future potential, all that is currently missing from our lives, and all that needs to be supplied and will be supplied so that we might accomplish God's purposes for us on this earth!

Consider for a few moments the vastness and variety of God's creation. All of the orbits of all the planets and stars and galaxies are known by God and governed by Him. He made both gnat and elephant, tadpole and whale. He made the great variety of flowers and birds, and made each unique so that even the aroma of a yellow rose is not the same as that of a red one. He made each of His creatures with unique qualities and abilities. I once had a redwood trellis that was eaten away in places by *ants*. Did you know that ants can bore their way into redwood—no human being has the ability to take a bite out of a tree, yet ants have that ability!

Consider for a few moments the intricacy of God's creation—all the systems and creatures exist in "balance" with one another. He made the spider to spin delicate webs, and the breezes to carry pollen from one plant to the next.

God controls it all—tides and orbits and the clash of atoms in the invisible realm.

And this is the God who created *you*. He knows you inside and out. And what He made, He can remake. What He created, He can refashion. What He caused to come into being, He can heal, restore, and mend.

- *How do you feel about the fact that Jesus knows everything about you?*

_____

_____

Created to Serve

Paul also wrote that we were created *for* Him. You were not created to serve the devil or to serve yourself alone. You were created to serve Jesus Christ. It also means that you were created to praise Him, worship Him, and bring glory to His name.

What does it mean for us to know that we were created by Christ and *for* Christ? It means that Christ Jesus has a plan for our lives. We do not need to wander aimlessly through life, without purpose or goals. God has a plan for us to fulfill. He has designed us to do a specific work on this earth for His purposes and His glory.

- *How do you feel about knowing that you were created FOR Christ Jesus?*

_____

_____

Finally, a key aspect of Jesus Christ being our "Creator" means that Jesus was not only present at the time of our physical, natural creation—our conception and birth—but He was present at the time we received Him as our Savior. He was present at our spiritual re-creation, the time when we were born again. He is the One who makes all things new in our lives, the One who regards us as a "new creation" with a spiritual nature that is completely different from our old sin nature. It is Jesus Christ who transforms us spiritually, and it is *for* Him that we are to live spiritually.

What the Word Says

He was in the beginning with God. All things were made through Him, and without Him nothing was made that was made. In Him was life. (John 1:2–4)

Jesus, the author and finisher of our faith. (Heb. 12:2)

If anyone is in Christ, he is a new creation; old things have passed away; behold, all things have become new. (2 Cor. 5:17)

What the Word Says to Me

_____

_____

_____

_____

_____

_____

_____

_____

_____

_____

_____

_____

• *In what ways are you feeling challenged in your spirit?*

_____

_____

• *What new insights do you have into the authority of Christ over your life?*

_____

_____

Jesus Christ Governs All Systems and Laws

Jesus Christ is not only the One who made you, but He is the One who governs all of the natural and spiritual systems and laws that impact your life.

He created all things "visible and invisible, whether thrones or dominions or principalities or powers" (Col. 1:16). This means that all natural laws were created by Him and continue to be governed by Him. He holds all things together by the power of His word! And not only laws that relate to the earth as we know it, but to the *processes* in the emotional and spiritual realm that govern our relationships and the effectiveness of our prayer and our faith. Jesus Christ is Lord of *all*.

Look again at Colossians 1:15–20 and this time, circle or highlight each time the word *all* appears:

> He is the image of the invisible God, the firstborn over all creation. For by Him all things were created that are in heaven and that are on earth, visible and invisible, whether thrones or dominions or principalities or powers. All things were created through Him and for Him. And He is before all things, and in Him all things consist. And He is the head of the body, the church, who is the beginning, the firstborn from the dead, that in all things He may have the preeminence. For it pleased the Father that in Him all the fullness should dwell, and by

Him to reconcile all things to Himself, by Him, whether things on earth or things in heaven, having made peace through the blood of His cross.

What does it mean to you and me to have *all* things governed by Jesus Christ? It means that all processes, procedures, systems, and "laws" are subject to Jesus Christ. He can use any method He desires to bring us the things we need. He can tap any resource and any "system" to bring us the power, ideas, information, courage, resources, help, energy, or creativity that may be necessary for us to fulfill God's plan for our lives.

- *How do you feel about Jesus Christ governing all things?*

_____

_____

- *What new insights do you have into Christ's sufficiency?*

_____

_____

What the Word Says

His Son, whom He has appointed heir of all things, through whom also He made the worlds; who being the brightness of His glory and the express image of His person, and upholding all things by the word of His power. (Heb. 1:2–3)

Therefore God also has highly exalted Him and given Him

What the Word Says to Me

_____

_____

_____

_____

_____

_____

_____

_____

_____

_____

the name which is above every
name, that at the name of
Jesus every knee should bow,
of those in heaven, and of
those on earth, and of those
under the earth, and that every
tongue should confess that
Jesus Christ is Lord, to the
glory of God the Father. (Phil.
2:9–11)

What More Could We Possibly Need?

If Jesus Christ is our Creator and knows everything about us, and if all the resources, systems, and laws of the universe are governed by Jesus Christ, what more could we possibly need than Christ? In what else could we possibly place our confidence?

The world tells us that we need many things to be successful and effective—a big bank account, a house in the right neighborhood, a college education, a job at the right firm, a perfect spouse and children, the right friends, designer clothes, the most expensive car, and even the right toothpaste to attract the opposite sex. God's Word says that you need only one thing for confidence and that is a relationship with Jesus Christ.

Our Response to His Sufficiency

Many people do not put their entire trust and confidence in Jesus Christ for one main reason: Satan has blinded them to the deity and power of Jesus Christ. Paul wrote to the Corinthians:

> Even if our gospel is veiled, it is veiled to those who are perishing, whose minds the god of this age has blinded,

who do not believe, lest the light of the gospel of the
glory of Christ, who is the image of God, should shine
on them. (2 Cor. 4:3–4)

When people are blinded to Christ's presence, nature, and
identity, and they do not fully recognize who He is, they tend
to make their own "gods." Such gods are always on their side,
always do what they want, and always approve of their desires.

Once we recognize fully, however, the nature, character, and
identity of God the Son, Jesus Christ, we are freed from striving to "work up" confidence and effectiveness.

Paul prayed for the Ephesians that this would be their
response to the sufficiency of Christ:

That the God of our Lord Jesus Christ, the Father of
glory, may give to you the spirit of wisdom and revelation in the knowledge of Him, the eyes of your
understanding being enlightened; that you may know
what is the hope of His calling, what are the riches of
the glory of His inheritance in the saints, and what is
the exceeding greatness of His power toward us who
believe. (1:17–19)

Note the three things Paul longs for them to have:

1. A complete understanding so they will know the *hope* of
   God's calling on their lives—in other words, they will know
   the future and the destiny that God built into their very
   creation.
2. The riches of their inheritance as believers in Christ
   Jesus—fully to know and receive all that Christ makes
   available to them to help them fulfill their God-given plan
   and purpose.
3. The greatness of Christ's power through the Holy Spirit
   to help them become, say, and do all that He desires for
   them to become, say, and do.

• *What new insights do you have into this passage from Ephesians?*

_____

_____

Jesus Christ truly is adequate for all things. He gives the motivation, the resources, and the power to accomplish all that needs to be accomplished. It is our view of Jesus that is inadequate. Ask the Lord today to enlarge your view of Jesus Christ—truly to see Him as the One who knows all about you, governs all things around you, and desires to bring about the fullness of your life.

• *In what ways are you feeling challenged in your spirit today?*

_____

_____

LESSON 5

ALL WE NEED TO LIVE A GODLY LIFE

What happens to a person when he or she receives Jesus Christ as Savior and is born again spiritually? Several things happen simultaneously:

- The person receives God's complete forgiveness—the old sin nature is replaced with a new nature that desires God's righteousness. All consequences for past sins are erased.
- The person receives the gift of eternal life with God, a heavenly home forever.
- The person usually experiences a deep and abiding sense of peace and joy, although this may come over time as the person realizes more and more what God has done for him.
- The person receives the Holy Spirit into his life.

It is this last aspect of our spiritual birth that is the focus for this lesson. The Holy Spirit—sent by Jesus to dwell within all those who believe in Him—is the One who enables us to live a godly life every day for the rest of our lives. The Holy Spirit, which is the very Spirit of Christ Himself imparted to us in an "unlimited form," is with us always. He is our sufficiency as we seek to walk in the footsteps of Jesus.

A Spiritual Transformation

Being "born again" involves a spiritual transformation. This transformation is as complete in the spiritual realm as the physical birth of a person. Just as a baby goes from being a fetus to an infant, so a person is changed spiritually from the old spiritual nature to the new nature when he accepts Jesus Christ as his Savior.

What is it about our spirit that is changed?

While God the Father is not made in *our* physical form, we nevertheless are made in *His* likeness. Genesis 1:26–27 says,

> Then God said, "Let Us make man in Our image, according to Our likeness;" . . . So God created man in His own image; in the image of God He created him; male and female He created them.

The part of us that is God-like is certainly not our body. The part of us that is made in God's image is our inner part—and very specifically, our ability to think, our ability to feel, and our free will with which we make decisions and choices. While we will never have the infinite power, wisdom, or love of God, we have been created in His image to manifest power, wisdom, and love. When we are born again, we *think* differently, we *feel* differently, and our *will* is changed so that we begin to think as God thinks, feel as God feels, and make decisions and choices as God would make them. We begin to love others as God loves them.

- *What difference has the Holy Spirit made in your life as a believer in Christ Jesus?*

_____

_____

The born-again person has an ability to respond *as God does* to any particular situation or circumstance. We, therefore, are made capable of saying what God would say and doing what God would do. We become a vessel in which and through which God might manifest His awesome power, wisdom, and love.

How is this possible? Because when we confess our sins to God and receive His forgiveness, we simultaneously receive His very presence into our lives in the form of the Holy Spirit. Jesus spoke about this when He said to His disciples, "You shall be baptized with the Holy Spirit . . . you shall receive power when the Holy Spirit has come upon you; and you shall be witnesses to Me in Jerusalem, and in all Judea and Samaria, and to the end of the earth" (Acts 1:5, 8).

Jesus also had this to say about the Holy Spirit—Jesus' very own Spirit—coming to be *in* us:

> I do not pray for these alone, but also for those who will believe in Me through their word; that they all may be one, as You, Father, are in Me, and I in You; that they also may be one in Us, that the world may believe that You sent Me. And the glory which You gave Me I have given them, that they may be one just as We are one: *I in them*, and You in Me; that they may be made perfect in one. (John 17:20–23, emphasis added)

One of the main themes of the apostle Paul's ministry was "Christ in me." He wrote and taught repeatedly about the Spirit residing within us, enabling us to live a godly life. As you read the three passages below, reflect on the difference the Holy Spirit makes in a believer's life:

> You are not in the flesh but in the Spirit, if indeed the Spirit of God dwells in you. Now if anyone does not have the Spirit of Christ, he is not His. And if Christ is in you, the body is dead because of sin, but the Spirit is

life because of righteousness. But if the Spirit of Him who raised Jesus from the dead dwells in you, He who raised Christ from the dead will also give life to your mortal bodies through His Spirit who dwells in you. (Rom. 8:9–11)

For as many as are led by the Spirit of God, these are sons of God. For you did not receive the spirit of bondage again to fear, but you received the Spirit of adoption by whom we cry out, "Abba, Father." (Rom. 8:14–15)

Do you not know that you are the temple of God and that the Spirit of God dwells in you? (1 Cor. 3:16)

• *What new insights do you have into these passages of Scripture about the Spirit of Christ Jesus dwelling in us?*

_____

_____

One of the most wonderful truths in the Bible is this: As a believer in Jesus Christ, you have been indwelled by the very Spirit of Christ Jesus. God the Holy Spirit dwells inside your mortal flesh!

What the Word Says	What the Word Says to Me
You . . . have put on the new man who is renewed in knowledge according to the image of Him who created him. (Col. 3:9–10)	_____
He made Him who knew no sin to be sin for us, that we might become the	_____

righteousness of God in Him.
(2 Cor. 5:21)

- -

- -

We have been delivered from
the law, having died to what we
were held by, so that we should
serve in the newness of the
Spirit and not in the oldness of
the letter. (Rom. 7:6)

- -

- -

- -

- -

- -

- -

The Seal of the Holy Spirit

The Holy Spirit functions to "seal" us into the life of Christ Jesus. In Bible times, a seal served two functions. First, a seal was used to secure a document or object. The Holy Spirit's presence in our life "seals" us, securing us from any attempts of the devil to claim our souls for eternity. We are marked as God's own forever once we are indwelled by the Holy Spirit. Nothing and nobody can cause the Holy Spirit to depart from our lives. His sealing of us is absolute and lasting.

Second, a seal in Bible times was used to declare the ownership of an object. Seals were individually made, and no two seals were alike. In the gospel of Mark, Jesus was asked whether the Jews should pay taxes to Rome. Jesus asked for a coin. He then said to them, using the coin as an example, "Render to Caesar the things that are Caesar's, and to God the things that are God's" (Mark 12:17). Jesus was saying that the person whose seal or "image" is on an item is the owner of the item. When the Holy Spirit places His seal on our lives, we are identified as belonging to Christ.

What the Word Says

What the Word Says to Me

Nevertheless the solid foundation of God stands, having this
seal: "The Lord knows those
who are His." (2 Tim. 2:19)

- -

- -

- -

- -

Now He who establishes us
with you in Christ and has
anointed us is God, who also
has sealed us and given us the
Spirit in our hearts as a guar-
antee. (2 Cor. 1:21–22)

Having believed, you were
sealed with the Holy Spirit of
promise. (Eph. 1:13)

And do not grieve the Holy
Spirit of God, by whom you
were sealed for the day of
redemption. (Eph. 4:30)

• *How do you feel about being "sealed" in Christ Jesus by the Holy Spirit?*

The Holy Spirit Convicts of Sin

Those who genuinely have been born again do not have a desire to sin. Their desire is to do the will of God the Father. Those who willfully choose to sin or to continue to sin deny the Lordship of Jesus Christ; they commit idolatry—choosing to follow and to put their trust in something or someone other than Christ Jesus. The apostle John wrote that those who have been born anew have a different "seed" in them from those who still have a sinful nature—they bear the "seed" of Jesus Christ and because of this, they desire purity, righteousness, and obedience. John wrote:

For this purpose the Son of God was manifested, that He might destroy the works of the devil. Whoever has been born of God does not sin, for His seed remains in him; and he cannot sin, because he has been born of God. (1 John 3:8–9)

This does not mean that a Christian *cannot* sin, but rather, that a Christian does not willfully choose to sin. As soon as a believer in Christ Jesus recognizes his sin, he seeks immediately to confess that sin, receive forgiveness for it, and to repent, which means to change one's will and to seek to obey God fully.

The Holy Spirit is quick to convict the believer of sin—not so that the believer's life might be miserable under a load of condemnation, but rather, so that the believer might quickly confess sin, be forgiven for it, and move forward in his life *without* guilt, shame, or feelings of condemnation. Furthermore, the Holy Spirit enables a believer to withstand future sinful temptations and to withstand evil.

- *Have you experienced the work of the Holy Spirit in your life to convict you of sin and help you withstand the temptation to sin? Have you noticed a change in your desire to sin since you accepted Christ into your life?*

What the Word Says	What the Word Says to Me
[Jesus said,] "And when He has come, He will convict the world of sin, and of righteousness, and of judgment: of sin, because they do not believe in Me; of righteousness, because I go to My Father and you see Me no more; of judgment,	_____ _____ _____ _____ _____ _____ _____

because the ruler of this world
is judged." (John 16:8–11)

Little children, let no one
deceive you. He who practices
righteousness is righteous, just
as He is righteous. He who
sins is of the devil, for the devil
has sinned from the beginning.
For this purpose the Son of
God was manifested, that He
might destroy the works of the
devil. (1 John 3:7–8)

- *In what ways are you feeling challenged in your spirit?*

_____

_____

The Holy Spirit Leads and Guides

In several passages of Scripture, Jesus refers to the Holy Spirit as the "Spirit of truth." The Holy Spirit leads us to decisions, choices, and an understanding of God's will that is "right" or true from God's perspective. He empowers us both to *know* and to *keep* God's commandments. In fact, John wrote that one of the ways we can know that the Holy Spirit dwells within a person is that the person keeps God's statutes (see 1 John 3:24).

The Holy Spirit leads us in such a way that over time, believing, saying, and doing the "right thing" become as natural to us as breathing. The more we rely upon the help of the Holy Spirit to guide us into all truth and to lead us into the path of God's perfect will, the more we take on the character of Christ and the more we automatically seek to do what is pleasing in God's sight. Stop to think for a moment—a mother bird doesn't *teach* its baby birds to build nests. Neither do mother squirrels teach baby squirrels that "winter's coming so it's time to gather and store food." God's creatures have a built-in instinct to do what must be done. So, too, the Holy Spirit becomes our built-in instinct for doing what is right in God's eyes. He is our Teacher and our Counselor.

• *Can you recall an experience in your life in which the Holy Spirit led you into a right decision or guided you into a right choice?*

_____

_____

• *In what ways has the Holy Spirit helped you to obey God's commandments?*

_____

_____

What the Word Says

[Jesus said,] "But the Helper, the Holy Spirit, whom the Father will send in My name, He will teach you all things, and bring to your remembrance all things that I said to you." (John 14:26)

[Jesus said,] "When the Helper comes, whom I shall send to you from the Father, the Spirit of truth who proceeds from the Father, He will testify of Me." (John 15:26)

[Jesus said,] "When He, the Spirit of truth, has come, He

What the Word Says to Me

_____

_____

_____

_____

_____

_____

_____

_____

_____

_____

_____

_____

_____

_____

_____

will guide you into all truth."
(John 16:13)

_____

_____

[Jesus said,] "If you abide in
My word, you are My disciples
indeed. And you shall know
the truth, and the truth shall
make you free." (John
8:31–32)

_____

_____

_____

_____

_____

_____

Now he who keeps His com-
mandments abides in Him,
and He in him. And by this we
know that He abides in us, by
the Spirit whom He has given
us. (1 John 3:24)

_____

_____

_____

_____

_____

_____

- *In what ways are you feeling challenged in your spirit?*

_____

_____

The Holy Spirit Makes Us Effective

The Holy Spirit makes our witness of Christ effective. As we noted at the beginning of this lesson, Jesus told His disciples that when they were baptized with the Holy Spirit, they would "receive power . . . and you shall be witnesses to Me" (Acts 1:8).

The Holy Spirit is the One who makes our prayers effective, who causes our sharing of the gospel to prick the conscience of the nonbeliever, and who causes our ministry efforts to meet needs in the lives of others. No person can save a soul, no person can heal a body, no person can make another person whole—but Christ Jesus can and does do these works *if we will be faithful in sharing God's love and the message of salvation* with those who need to receive it.

What the Word Says

[Jesus said about the Spirit of truth,] "He will glorify Me, for He will take of what is Mine and declare it to you . . . Whatever you ask the Father in My name He will give you. Until now you have asked nothing in My name. Ask, and you will receive, that your joy may be full." (John 16:14, 23–24)

[Jesus said,] "Most assuredly, I say to you, he who believes in Me, the works that I do he will do also; and greater works than these he will do, because I go to My Father. And whatever you ask in My name, that I will do, that the Father may be glorified in the Son. If you ask anything in My name, I will do it." (John 14:12–14)

Likewise the Spirit also helps in our weaknesses. For we do not know what we should pray for as we ought, but the Spirit Himself makes intercession for us with groanings which cannot be uttered. Now He who searches the hearts knows what

What the Word Says to Me

----

the mind of the Spirit is,
because He makes intercession
for the saints according to the
will of God. (Rom. 8:26–27)

_____
_____
_____
_____

- *In what ways are you feeling challenged in your spirit?*

_____

_____

Inviting the Holy Spirit to Do His Work

How is it that we are to respond to God the Holy Spirit dwelling with us? By inviting Him to *be* our sufficiency day by day.

The reason so many Christians seem to stumble and falter in their Christian walk is because they simply are too proud to acknowledge that they *need* God the Holy Spirit at all times and in all decisions and choices. The truth is, we can't do *anything* by ourselves in our own human strength. We cannot make our heart beat one additional beat or add one fraction of an inch to our height. The Holy Spirit within us *is* life. It is up to us to invite Him to do His work in us and through us.

- *What new insights do you have into the sufficiency of Christ Jesus, through the power of the Holy Spirit, to help you live a godly life and to be an effective witness for the gospel?*

_____

_____

ALL WE NEED FOR TOTAL PROVISION

Have you ever stopped to consider that nobody else can do what Jesus Christ can do? Nobody else can save a soul, deliver a person from evil, heal the body, mind, or emotions, create abiding and lasting peace and joy in the human heart, or make a person whole. Human efforts can help set the stage for Jesus Christ to do His work, but no human being can do what Christ can do!

Isn't it amazing, then, that we *think* we can meet our physical and material needs apart from Jesus? So many people are attempting to do just that! Even many Christians seem to believe that Jesus Christ can meet all spiritual needs, but that when it comes to the meeting of their physical, emotional, or material needs, they need to look to something other than or something in addition to Him.

The fact is, however, that none of us can create any form of lasting provision or security for ourselves in the physical or material realm. Stock markets rise and fall, jobs are secured and lost, clients come and go, vendors change, children grow up and leave home, loved ones die, government policies and laws are revised, methods change, crime occurs, disease strikes . . . nothing stays the same forever except Jesus Christ.

A second major truth about the sufficiency of Jesus Christ is this: There is no need too great or too small for Jesus Christ to meet it *completely.* We can never face a problem Jesus can't solve, a question He can't answer, or a need He can't fulfill.

- *In reflecting back on your life, in what have you put your trust for security or provision other than Christ Jesus? What were the results?*

_____

_____

- *In reflecting back on your life, can you cite any area of need that Jesus Christ was incapable of meeting?*

_____

_____

External and Internal Provision

The New Testament writers were very clear in their understanding that Jesus Christ would meet *all* of their needs, both external and internal. The apostle Paul wrote to the Philippians, "My God shall supply all your need according to His riches in glory by Christ Jesus" (Phil. 4:19).

Paul did not place any qualifications upon the supply made available to us through Christ Jesus. In other words, Paul did not say that Christ Jesus would only meet spiritual needs, or physical needs, or financial and material needs. Paul wrote that Christ Jesus meets *all* manner and type of need.

- *Thinking about your life as a whole, list some of the needs that you have today—physical, emotional, relational, financial, material, spiritual.*

_____

_____

If a person is truly honest with himself, he will admit that the things he desires most in life are the intangibles that cannot be purchased and are not man-made: health, loving relationships, fulfillment and meaning in life. Jesus Christ is ultimately the number one Source for all things that matter the most to us:

- Wisdom and understanding
- Total health—spirit, mind, and body
- Feelings of belonging and loving relationships with others
- Fulfilling and meaningful ministry to others
- Blessings that are material, emotional, and spiritual
- Hope, peace, joy, and unconditional love
- Spiritual insights and intimacy with God the Father
- Healthy self-esteem and a feeling of worthiness in knowing we are a beloved child of God
- Deliverance from evil
- Forgiveness of sin
- Freedom from guilt and shame

It is when we recognize that Christ Jesus living in us makes all things possible for us that we are able to say with the apostle Paul,

> I have learned in whatever state I am, to be content: I know how to be abased, and I know how to abound. Everywhere and in all things I have learned both to be full and to be hungry, both to abound and to suffer need. I can do all things through Christ who strengthens me. (Phil. 4:11–13)

As long as we are relying on ourselves or on any source other than Christ Jesus to be our provision and our security, we will not be content. Why? Because deep inside we know that all man-made systems, including our own self-efforts, ultimately fall short or fail. Beauty fades, status changes, fame slides away, power wanes, possessions rust and rot. Only what Christ Jesus provides is lasting and sure. Why? Because He is eternal and trustworthy. Nobody can supply our needs as Jesus Christ can supply them!

What the Word Says	What the Word Says to Me
I also, after I heard of your faith in the Lord Jesus and your love for all the saints, do not cease to give thanks for you, making mention of you in my prayers: that the God of our Lord Jesus Christ, the Father of glory, may give to you the spirit of wisdom and revelation in the knowledge of Him, the eyes of your understanding being enlightened; that you may know what is the hope of His calling, what are the riches of the glory of His inheritance in the saints. (Eph. 1:15–18)	_____ _____ _____ _____ _____ _____ _____ _____ _____ _____ _____ _____ _____ _____ _____ _____ _____
That in the ages to come He might show the exceeding riches of His grace in His kindness toward us in Christ Jesus. (Eph. 2:7)	_____ _____ _____ _____ _____
Jesus Christ is the same yesterday, today, and forever. (Heb. 13:8)	_____ _____ _____

A Fresh and Constant Supply

What Jesus gives to us is always fresh and individually designed. He never gives a stale, secondhand, or warmed-over blessing. Many people seem to believe that God has a certain number of blessings for a person, and once they have used up their allotment, no more blessings are available. That is totally contrary to what the Bible teaches! God's riches are unlimited—His storehouse is infinite and His mercy toward us is daily, vibrant, life-giving, and steadfast in its supply.

The fact is, we never outgrow our neediness. We never become so mature physically, emotionally, or spiritually that we no longer have needs. Just as we have a need for food, water, and fresh air on a daily basis, so we have a constant, ever-present need for God's love, care, comfort, forgiveness, mercy, and security. Jesus knows that every person has a constant need for those things that only He can give. That's why He taught His disciples,

> I am the vine, you are the branches. He who abides in Me, and I in him, bears much fruit; for without Me you can do nothing . . . If you abide in Me, and My words abide in you, you will ask what you desire, and it shall be done for you. By this My Father is glorified, that you bear much fruit; so you will be My disciples. As the Father loved Me, I also have loved you; abide in My love. (John 15:5, 7–9)

- *What new insights do you have into the provision that Christ Jesus supplies to us as we "abide" in Him, in His words, and in His love?*

_____

_____

What the Word Says	**What the Word Says to Me**
This I recall to my mind,	_____
Therefore I have hope.	_____
Through the LORD's mercies	_____
we are not consumed,	_____

Because His compassions fail
not.
They are new every morning;
Great is Your faithfulness.
"The LORD is my portion,"
says my soul,
"Therefore I hope in Him!"
(Lam. 3:21–24)

[Jesus said,] "Are not five sparrows sold for two copper
coins? And not one of them is
forgotten before God. But the
very hairs of your head are all
numbered. Do not fear therefore; you are of more value
than many sparrows." (Luke
12:6–7)

[Jesus said,] "Consider the
lilies, how they grow: they neither toil nor spin; and yet I say
to you, even Solomon in all his
glory was not arrayed like one
of these. If then God so clothes
the grass, which today is in the
field and tomorrow is thrown
into the oven, how much more
will He clothe you, O you of
little faith?" (Luke 12:27–28)

Why Needs Aren't Met

There are many reasons why our needs aren't met as quickly
or in the way we desire. Perhaps the foremost reason is that we

do not truly trust Jesus Christ to meet our needs in His way, in His timing, and according to His purposes. As James wrote, "You do not have because you do not ask" (James 4:2). Do not let your pride, ego, arrogance, or concern about pomp and prestige keep you from humbly asking God for what you need.

Furthermore, when we ask, we are to ask with faith:

> Let him ask in faith, with no doubting, for he who doubts is like a wave of the sea driven and tossed by the wind. For let not that man suppose that he will receive anything from the Lord; he is a double-minded man, unstable in all his ways. (James 1:6–8)

Two other factors often keep us from receiving what we need:

1. *Sin.* We willfully choose to do things our way rather than God's way; we follow our own "law" rather than follow God's commandments.
2. *Misplaced Motives.* We desire things that are not pleasing to God or we desire to manipulate others.

God is under no obligation to answer requests that are contrary to His plan and purpose for our lives. He will not contribute to our sin, our desire to manipulate other people, or our desires that are rooted in self-pride.

What the Word Says	What the Word Says to Me
When the disciples saw it, they marveled, saying, "How did the fig tree wither away so soon?" So Jesus answered and said to them, "Assuredly, I say to you, if you have faith and do not doubt, you will not only do	------------------------------ ------------------------------ ------------------------------ ------------------------------ ------------------------------ ------------------------------ ------------------------------

what was done to the fig tree, but also if you say to this mountain, 'Be removed and be cast into the sea,' it will be done. And whatever things you ask in prayer, believing, you will receive." (Matt. 21:20–22)

[Jesus taught,] "Ask, and it will be given to you; seek, and you will find; knock, and it will be opened to you." (Matt. 7:7)

Now this is the confidence that we have in Him, that if we ask anything according to His will, He hears us. And if we know that He hears us, whatever we ask, we know that we have the petitions that we have asked of Him. (1 John 5:14–15)

And whatever we ask we receive from Him, because we keep His commandments and do those things that are pleasing in His sight. (1 John 3:22)

[Jesus said,] "If you keep My commandments, you will abide in My love, just as I have kept My Father's commandments and abide in His love." (John 15:10)

Covetousness and Greediness

Greediness and covetousness can easily invade our desire for things we think we need. Always ask yourself, "Is this something that *God* desires for me to have?" We are wise to ask only for those things that are for our eternal good and for the benefit of others around us.

What the Word Says	What the Word Says to Me
Let your conduct be without covetousness; be content with such things as you have. For He Himself has said, "I will never leave you nor forsake you." (Heb. 13:5)	_____ _____ _____ _____ _____ _____
You ask and do not receive, because you ask amiss, that you may spend it on your pleasures. (James 4:3)	_____ _____ _____ _____

• *In what ways are you feeling challenged in your spirit?*

_____

_____

His Supply Is Abundant

Jesus said, "I have come that they may have life, and that they may have it more abundantly" (John 10:10). God is not stingy. He does not supply the needs of His beloved children with meagerness. His love and mercy and provision are overflowing.

When the Lord revealed Himself to Moses, He made a statement to Moses about His own character and nature:

And the LORD passed before him and proclaimed, "The LORD, the LORD God, merciful and gracious, longsuffering, and *abounding in goodness and truth*, keeping mercy for thousands, forgiving iniquity and transgression and sin." (Ex. 34:6–7, emphasis added)

There is no end to the goodness that God desires to pour out on you as His beloved child. As you grow in your obedience to Him, you will experience an increasing supply of His blessing. Out of His infinite supply, He pours an infinite blessing!

- *How do you feel about God's ability and desire to supply all your needs with a fresh and overflowing supply?*

_____

_____

What the Word Says	What the Word Says to Me
"Try Me now in this,"	_____
Says the LORD of hosts,	_____
"If I will not open for you the	_____
windows of heaven	_____
And pour out for you such	_____
blessing	_____
That there will not be room	_____
enough to receive it.	_____
And I will rebuke the devourer	_____
for your sakes,	_____
So that he will not destroy the	_____
fruit of your ground,	_____
Nor shall the vine fail to bear	_____
fruit for you in the field,"	_____
Says the LORD of hosts;	_____

"And all nations will call you
blessed,
For you will be a delightful
land." (Mal. 3:10–12)

And the grace of our Lord was
exceedingly abundant, with
faith and love which are in
Christ Jesus. (1 Tim. 1:14)

Now to Him who is able to do
exceedingly abundantly above
all that we ask or think,
according to the power that
works in us, to Him be glory in
the church by Christ Jesus to
all generations, forever and
ever. Amen. (Eph. 3:20–21)

Our Response to His Provision

Our response to the totally sufficient provision made available through Christ Jesus should be one of thanksgiving and praise. Paul wrote to the Colossians,

> As you therefore have received Christ Jesus the Lord, so walk in Him, rooted and built up in Him and established in the faith, as you have been taught, abounding in it with thanksgiving. (Col. 2:6–7)

We are to be thankful and to praise the Lord *not only when all of our need is met* but also when we are experiencing lack, knowing that Jesus Christ has met, is meeting, and will meet all of our need. No need we ever have is a surprise to Jesus Christ. He has known everything we will need to fulfill our purpose in life from the moment we were created, and along with our creation, Jesus Christ created the full provision for the meeting of all our needs. Therefore, we can thank and praise the Lord for meeting our needs even if we don't yet see or experience the reality of His provision. As the writer to the Hebrews stated so well, "Now faith is the substance of things hoped for, the evidence of things not seen" (Heb. 11:1).

As you read the passage of Scripture below, note how thankful Paul was for the offering that the Corinthians had entrusted to him.

> Now may He who supplies seed to the sower, and bread for food, supply and multiply the seed you have sown and increase the fruits of your righteousness, while you are enriched in everything for all liberality, which causes thanksgiving through us to God. For the administration of this service not only supplies the needs of the saints, but also is abounding through many thanksgivings to God. (2 Cor. 9:10–12)

The proper response to God's sufficiency is always praise and thanksgiving!

What the Word Says	What the Word Says to Me
In everything by prayer and supplication, with thanksgiving, let your requests be made known to God. (Phil. 4:6)	_____ _____ _____ _____
Thanks be to God, who gives us the victory through our Lord Jesus Christ. (1 Cor. 15:57)	_____ _____ _____
Now thanks be to God who	_____

always leads us in triumph in
Christ, and through us diffuses
the fragrance of His knowledge
in every place. (2 Cor. 2:14)

Thanks be to God for His
indescribable gift! (2 Cor.
9:15)

- *What new insights do you have into the provision made available to us through Jesus Christ, and about how to receive His provision for all your needs?*

  _____

  _____

- *In what ways are you feeling challenged in your spirit?*

  _____

  _____

ALL WE NEED FOR OUR IDENTITY AND PERFECTION

Have you ever stopped to consider that you are the workmanship of God? He is the One who is making you, molding you, fashioning you, chipping away the rough edges in you, and *perfecting* you!

So many people in our world today are struggling to "make" themselves. They are attempting to achieve success totally on their own efforts. In some cases, people are using others to try to achieve the success they desire. The Bible teaches us, however, that it is God who defines us and perfects us. It is God who has a plan for us, as the prophet Jeremiah declared: "For I know the thoughts that I think toward you, says the LORD, thoughts of peace and not of evil, to give you a future and a hope" (Jer. 29:11)

The Lord created each of us with a future! He had a good plan and purpose in mind at the instant of our creation. And, as we rely on His sufficiency, He will work diligently, tirelessly, and constantly to bring that plan and purpose to full fruition!

- *As you reflect back over your life, what are some of the ways in which you have attempted to "make" your own life?*

_____

_____

What the Word Says

Thus says the LORD . . . "I will set My eyes on them for good, and I will bring them back to this land; I will build them and not pull them down, and I will plant them and not pluck them up. Then I will give them a heart to know Me, that I am the LORD; and they shall be My people, and I will be their God." (Jer. 24:5–7)

For we are His workmanship, created in Christ Jesus for good works, which God prepared beforehand that we should walk in them. (Eph. 2:10)

But we have this treasure in earthen vessels, that the excellence of the power may be of God and not of us. (2 Cor. 4:7)

What the Word Says to Me

_____

_____

_____

_____

_____

_____

_____

_____

_____

_____

_____

_____

_____

_____

_____

_____

_____

_____

_____

- *How do you feel about the truth that God has a "good plan" and a "good future" for you?*

_____

_____

No More Self-Striving

For years, I felt as if I were on something of a spiritual and emotional roller coaster in my relationship with the Lord. I had ups and downs, highs and lows, and often my emotions just seemed to go round and round—some things that I thought I had dealt with reappeared again and again, which was both discouraging and frustrating. In many ways, I felt locked into a relationship with the Lord that I really didn't enjoy very much.

And then I faced the fact that my problem was not created by the Lord, but by *me*. I was trying to make my own joy, my own peace, my own fulfillment, my own success, my own sense of well-being. I was striving to do what no person can do—create inner health and wholeness. When I came face-to-face with the great truth that the apostle Paul proclaims again and again in his letters—"Christ in me, I in Christ"— I found a new freedom and genuine joy in my relationship with Jesus Christ that was far beyond anything I had ever experienced.

The "Christ in me" aspect of our Christian life is what qualifies and prepares us for an eternal life in heaven. As the apostle Paul wrote to the Colossians, "Christ in you, the hope of glory" (Col. 1:27).

The "I in Christ" aspect of our Christian life is what prepares us to live a victorious life of purpose on this earth. Paul wrote to the Corinthians: "He who establishes us with you *in Christ* and has anointed us is God" (2 Cor. 1:21, emphasis added).

It is a great spiritual mystery that Christ Jesus dwells within us and we within Him. Paul readily admits that to the Colossians, saying, "To them God willed to make known what are the riches of the glory of this mystery among the Gentiles" (Col. 1:27). This truth about our relationship with Christ Jesus cannot be understood totally with the rational mind. Those who are not Christians *cannot* understand the relationship a believer has with Christ and we should never expect a nonbeliever to be able to understand this mystery with his mind. It is a spiritual truth that is understood only from the perspective of faith, or "believing." It is on the basis of our believing that Christ indwells us and we dwell in Him.

Christ dwelling within us becomes our *identity*, and it is His presence within us that leads to our *perfection*. We no longer belong to ourselves. We no longer are responsible for fashioning ourselves or making ourselves. We are under Christ's authority, we are His responsibility, we are totally subject to His will. He lives His life through us, and in the process, He transforms us and builds us up so that we feel tremendous joy, satisfaction, and fulfillment.

The Christian life is not a life of self-effort, but rather, it is allowing Jesus to live through us. Consider the difference between an artesian well and a pump. A pump requires effort and energy to pull the water up from the earth. In an artesian well or natural fountain, the water bubbles up of its own accord. No effort on the part of man is required. In like manner, when we trust Jesus Christ to be sufficient for all things in our lives, His Spirit bubbles up in us like a river of living water (See John 7:37–39). We do not need to strive to "work up" our faith; rather, we let His presence fill us and flow through us.

- *In your life, have you had experiences or times when you truly allowed the Holy Spirit to move "through" you to minister to others?*

_____

_____

What the Word Says

[Jesus said,] "Come to Me, all you who labor and are heavy

What the Word Says to Me

- -

- -

laden, and I will give you rest.
Take My yoke upon you and
learn from Me, for I am gentle
and lowly in heart, and you
will find rest for your souls.
For My yoke is easy and My
burden is light." (Matt.
11:28–30)

Jesus stood and cried out, saying, "If anyone thirsts, let him
come to Me and drink. He
who believes in Me, as the
Scripture has said, out of his
heart will flow rivers of living
water." But this He spoke con-
cerning the Spirit, whom those
believing in Him would
receive. (John 7:37–39)

You are not in the flesh but in
the Spirit, if indeed the Spirit
of God dwells in you. (Rom.
8:9)

Conformed to Christ

Paul wrote to the Romans of the plan of God for every
believer, saying,

> For whom He foreknew, He also predestined to be con-
> formed to the image of His Son, that He might be the
> firstborn among many brethren. Moreover whom He
> predestined, these He also called; whom He called, these
> He also justified; and whom He justified, these He also
> glorified. (Rom. 8:29–30)

You are "in process"! So is every other believer in Christ Jesus. We are not instantly made perfect when we accept Jesus Christ as our Savior. As the familiar bumper sticker says, "Christians aren't perfect, just forgiven." It is *as* we continue to put our trust in Jesus Christ to be the Lord of our lives that *He* does a perfecting, refining work in us. The terms Paul uses are *conform* and *justifies*.

"To conform" means to fashion something so that it is in exact likeness to a pattern. Jesus is the pattern. The Holy Spirit is making us so that we are *like* Jesus in our attitude, our reliance upon God the Father, our mercy, love, words, and behavior. To be conformed to Christ means that we become more and more like Jesus Christ day by day, making the choices and decisions that Jesus would make if He were living and walking through the circumstances and situations we face daily.

What does it mean to be justified? One of the meanings of the word *justify* is to "line up." When a printer justifies type he lines up the type so that the left margin is even and the right margin is even—as we see in most newspaper columns. When we accept Jesus as our Savior, God embarks upon a process of "lining us up" with the character and nature of Christ, making us more and more like Jesus every day for the rest of our lives. The Holy Spirit operates as the agent of re-creation and transformation in our lives. He is the One who molds us into the person God designed us to be.

The end result of our "justification" is our glorification—the more we are like Jesus Christ, the more we bring glory to Him and the greater His glory is revealed through us. The perfecting process brings us into genuine conformity to the nature and spiritual likeness of Jesus.

- *What new insights do you have into Romans 8:29–30?*

_____

_____

What the Word Says

What the Word Says to Me

The LORD will perfect that
which concerns me;
Your mercy, O LORD, endures
forever;
Do not forsake the works of
Your hands. (Ps. 138:8)

_____
_____
_____
_____
_____
_____

Let us go on to perfection.
(Heb. 6:1)

_____
_____

And He Himself gave some
to be apostles, some
prophets, some evangelists,
and some pastors and teachers, for the equipping of the
saints for the work of ministry, for the edifying of the
body of Christ, till we all
come to the unity of the faith
and of the knowledge of the
Son of God, to a perfect
man, to the measure of the
stature of the fullness of
Christ. (Eph. 4:11–13)

_____
_____
_____
_____
_____
_____
_____
_____
_____
_____
_____
_____
_____
_____

If we love one another, God
abides in us, and His love has
been perfected in us. (1 John
4:12)

_____
_____
_____
_____

Now may the God of peace . . .
make you complete in every
good work to do His will,
working in you what is well

_____
_____
_____
_____

pleasing in His sight, through
Jesus Christ. (Heb. 13:20–21)

_____

_____

- *In what ways are you feeling challenged in your spirit?*

_____

_____

Perfection Involves a "Breaking" Process

A "breaking process" is sometimes required for us to be perfected. Too often we look at the difficult times in our lives and ask, "Where is God? Why doesn't God do something about this circumstance or situation?" The fact is, God is present and He *is* doing something! The better questions to ask are these: "*What* is it, Lord, that You are trying to teach me through this? *What* is it that You are trying to change in me?"

- *In your life have you ever had an experience in which you felt the Lord was "breaking" you in order to bring about a positive change?*

_____

_____

What the Word Says

The word which came to Jeremiah from the LORD, saying: "Arise and go down to the potter's house, and there I will cause you to hear My words." Then I went down to the potter's house, and there he was, making something at the wheel. And the vessel that he made of clay was marred in the

What the Word Says to Me

_____
_____
_____
_____
_____
_____
_____
_____
_____
_____

hand of the potter; so he made
it again into another vessel, as
it seemed good to the potter to
make. Then the word of the
LORD came to me, saying: "O
house of Israel, can I not do
with you as this potter?" says
the LORD. "Look, as the clay is
in the potter's hand, so are you
in My hand." (Jer. 18:1–6)

[Jesus said,] "Every branch in
Me that does not bear fruit He
takes away; and every branch
that bears fruit He prunes, that
it may bear more fruit." (John
15:2)

Perfection Involves a Transformation in Our Thinking

As we are conformed to Jesus Christ, we begin to desire more and more to be like Him—to feel what He felt for other people and to love as He loved, to think what He thought and to apply the Scriptures as He applied them. The more we seek to think the very thoughts of Jesus, the more our minds are renewed by the Holy Spirit. We have a new and increasingly great ability to understand the Bible when we read it. We have new insights into what God is doing in our lives, in the lives of others, and in the world as a whole. Paul wrote to the Romans,

> And do not be conformed to this world, but be transformed by the renewing of your mind, that you may prove what is that good and acceptable and perfect will of God. (Rom. 12:2)

The transformation of our minds means that over time, we have a different "worldview." We see things from God's point of view. We desire only to know and to do God's will, because we have a new understanding that God's truth is lasting and eternally beneficial.

- *What new insights do you have into Romans 12:2?*

  _____

  _____

- *Reflecting back over your life before and after you accepted Jesus Christ as your Savior, how has your "thinking" changed? In what ways has your mind been transformed?*

  _____

  _____

Perfection Involves a "Putting Off and Putting On" Process

Paul described this remaking process to the Colossians in this way: Some aspects of our nature we are to "put off"—just as we would take off dirty, tattered clothing, and other aspects of Christ's nature we are to "put on." He encouraged the Colossians, "Set your mind on things above, not on things on the earth" (Col. 3:2). He then went on to write,

> But now you yourselves are to put off all these: anger, wrath, malice, blasphemy, filthy language out of your mouth. Do not lie to one another, since you have put off the old man with his deeds, and have put on the new man who is renewed in knowledge according to the image of Him who created him . . .

> Therefore, as the elect of God, holy and beloved, put on tender mercies, kindness, humility, meekness, longsuffering; bearing with one another, and forgiving one

another, if anyone has a complaint against another, even as Christ forgave you, so you also must do. But above all these things put on love, which is the bond of perfection. (Col. 3:8–10, 12–14)

Our part, through an act of our will and as an expression of our faith, is to *choose* not to engage in sinful behaviors and to *choose* instead to pursue righteous attitudes and behaviors. We do the choosing, and then the Holy Spirit gives us both the courage and the ability to follow through and act on our decisions. The Holy Spirit empowers us to obey once we have made our choice to obey God.

• *What new insights do you have into Colossians 3:8–14?*

_____

_____

What the Word Says	What the Word Says to Me
This is the covenant that I will make with them after those days, says the LORD: I will put My laws into their hearts, and in their minds I will write them. (Heb. 10:16)	_____ _____ _____ _____ _____ _____
Blessed is the man Who walks not in the counsel of the ungodly, Nor stands in the path of sinners, Nor sits in the seat of the scornful; But his delight is in the law of the LORD, And in His law he meditates day and night.	_____ _____ _____ _____ _____ _____ _____ _____ _____

He shall be like a tree
Planted by the rivers of water,
That brings forth its fruit in its
season,
Whose leaf also shall not
wither;
And whatever he does shall
prosper. (Ps. 1:1–3)

Finally, brethren, whatever
things are true, whatever things
are noble, whatever things are
just, whatever things are pure,
whatever things are lovely,
whatever things are of good
report, if there is any virtue
and if there is anything praise-
worthy—meditate on these
things. The things which you
learned and received and
heard and saw in me, these do,
and the God of peace will be
with you. (Phil. 4:8–9)

- *In what ways are you feeling challenged in your spirit?*

Perfection Involves a Building-Up Process

The perfection process in us is not only a "breaking and remaking" process, but a process of "building up." Those parts of us that are in need of remaking, the Lord breaks. Those aspects of our lives that are good in God's sight are the aspects that the Lord strengthens, fortifies, and builds up.

The Holy Spirit is the *Master of edification,* which is a term the Bible uses for the building up of a person's character and spirit.

A number of passages in the Bible use the analogy of our bodies as a building or a temple of the Holy Spirit. The building process is an orderly one. A firm, well-laid foundation is essential for a building to be strong—our foundation is Jesus Christ and the Word of God. Alignment of all aspects of a building is necessary for the building to be strong—the Cornerstone of our faith, Jesus Christ, enables us to come into proper alignment and to be "fitted together" well.

The building-up process always involves our relationships with others. We are never made perfect in a vacuum. God always uses other people as instruments to sand away and chisel our flaws, to teach us and counsel us with wisdom, and to build us up emotionally. God is not only giving you an identity as a person, but He is also putting you into a fellowship of believers so that, with others, you have an identity as His body. Your faith does not exist or operate apart from others; you are part of the church as a whole.

- *In your life, can you cite instances or ways in which the Holy Spirit has helped you to increase or strengthen your natural God-given abilities and talents?*

  _____

  _____

- *How has the Lord used other people to bring about your identity and your perfection in Christ Jesus?*

  _____

  _____

What the Word Says	What the Word Says to Me
Having been built on the foundation of the apostles and	_____ _____

prophets, Jesus Christ Himself
being the chief cornerstone, in
whom the whole building,
being fitted together, grows
into a holy temple in the Lord,
in whom you also are being
built together for a dwelling
place of God in the Spirit.
(Eph. 2:20–22)

Speaking the truth in love . . .
grow up in all things into Him
who is the head—Christ—from
whom the whole body, joined
and knit together by what
every joint supplies, according
to the effective working by
which every part does its
share, causes growth of the
body for the edifying of itself
in love. (Eph. 4:15–16)

Therefore comfort each other
and edify one another.
(1 Thess. 5:11)

As you therefore have received
Christ Jesus the Lord, so walk
in Him, rooted and built up in
Him and established in the
faith, as you have been taught.
(Col. 2:6–7)

- *In what ways are you feeling challenged in your spirit?*

_____

_____

- *What new insights do you have into Christ Jesus as the sufficiency for our growth and perfection?*

_____

_____

ALL WE NEED TO HAVE MEANING FOR OUR LIVES

The Greek culture in which many of the first-century Christians lived was a world very much like the one in which we live. People were greatly concerned with the meaning of life. Lengthy discussions and debates focused on the age-old questions, "Who am I? Why am I here? What is life all about? Where does it all end?"

The apostle Paul addressed these concerns in his letter to the Colossians:

> Beware lest anyone cheat you through philosophy and empty deceit, according to the tradition of men, according to the basic principles of the world, and not according to Christ. For in Him dwells all the fullness of the Godhead bodily; and you are complete in Him, who is the head of all principality and power. (Col. 2:8–10)

I want you to notice several things in this passage. First, Paul says that he does not want the Colossians to be "cheated" by the world's philosophy. This word is translated in some versions of the Bible as "captured"—in the Greek language the term is actually two words that literally mean "taken away as booty" and in the process, being "deprived of freedom." Paul does not want the Colossians to become slaves to the world or *prisoners of Satan* because they have been enticed to believe the wrong things. He does not want them to be cheated of genuine spiritual freedom.

- *Have you ever been held back, kept in a type of bondage, or hindered in your walk with Christ by an error in your thinking?*

_____

_____

What the Word Says	What the Word Says to Me
[Jesus said,] "And you shall know the truth, and the truth shall make you free." (John 8:32)	_____ _____ _____ _____
I have no greater joy than to hear that my children walk in truth. (3 John 4)	_____ _____ _____
For this is good and acceptable in the sight of God our Savior, who desires all men to be saved and to come to the knowledge of the truth. (1 Tim. 2:3–4)	_____ _____ _____ _____ _____

- *In what ways are you feeling challenged in your spirit?*

_____

_____

Your Spiritual Freedom Can Be Taken from You

Paul warned that we can be cheated of our spiritual freedom if we buy into the "philosophy" of the world. Philosophy is concerned with three main things:

1. *The existence of man*, which leads us to ask, "Who am I?"
2. *The source of all things*, which leads us to ask, "Where did I come from?"
3. *The purpose of all things*, which leads us to ask, "Why am I here?"

A concern with the source and purpose of all things leads to a concern about the conclusion of all things and what system of rewards and punishments may be in effect, which in turn leads us to ask, "Where does it all end?"

Every religion on earth attempts to answer these philosophical questions in some way, and often very elaborately. Paul admonished the Colossians not to be caught up in vast systems of philosophical belief, but rather, to stick with the simplicity of the gospel:

1. You are a beloved child of God, made in His image.
2. You are a creation of God, born again by the power of the Holy Spirit at work in your life.
3. You were destined by God from your creation to be conformed to the image of Christ and to fulfill God's unique plan and purpose for you on this earth.

As for the end of all things, the Bible teaches plainly that God gives everlasting life to those who believe in Jesus Christ (see John 3:16) and that He will reward all believers for what they do to further the kingdom of God on this earth.

How often, however, do we find people who try to make the truth of God more complicated than this? They add long lists of things a person must do to find meaning in life and to attain a good life in the world to come. They add to the gospel, and then add more to the gospel, until very often the gospel has all but disappeared from their teaching.

In the case of false religions, the performance of rituals is put in place of faith in the gospel. Those who deny the gospel and propose something in its place are guilty of "empty deceit." What they proclaim leads to nothing and has no bearing on eternal life. It may sound good. It may even produce a warm emotional feeling. But in the end, the teaching has no consequence for good, no lasting fruit. What such teachers teach is actually a lie that detracts and leads a person away from the truth.

Paul says about both philosophy and empty deceit: Don't be cheated! Don't be captured!

- *In your life, have you ever been led astray by those who would seek to add something to the gospel, or replace the gospel with another system of belief?*

_____

_____

What the Word Says

There were also false prophets among the people, even as there will be false teachers among you, who will secretly bring in destructive heresies, even denying the Lord who bought them, and bring on themselves swift destruction . . . By covetousness they will exploit you with deceptive words. (2 Peter 2:1, 3)

They shall teach My people

What the Word Says to Me

_____

_____

_____

_____

_____

_____

_____

_____

_____

_____

_____

_____

the difference between the holy and the unholy, and cause them to discern between the unclean and the clean. (Ezek. 44:23)

[Jesus taught,] "Beware of false prophets, who come to you in sheep's clothing, but inwardly they are ravenous wolves. You will know them by their fruits. Do men gather grapes from thornbushes or figs from thistles? Even so, every good tree bears good fruit, but a bad tree bears bad fruit . . . Therefore by their fruits you will know them." (Matt. 7:15–17, 20)

And daily in the temple, and in every house, they did not cease teaching and preaching Jesus as the Christ. (Acts 5:42)

Let the word of Christ dwell in you richly in all wisdom, teaching and admonishing one another in psalms and hymns and spiritual songs. (Col. 3:16)

• *In what ways are you feeling challenged in your spirit?*

Avoiding the False Traditions of Men

Paul also warned the Colossians against "the tradition of men, according to the basic principles of the world" (2:8). At the time Paul was writing, four main streams of thought were prevalent among both the Gentiles and the Greek-influenced Jews:

1. *Legalism,* a strict by-the-book approach to the code of law with little concern for the biblical "spirit of the law." Jesus referred to this legalism as "the tradition of the elders." The Law of Moses was no longer considered sufficient, but rather, an elaborate system of laws that *interpreted* the Law of Moses was called the law. These laws determined, for example, how far a person could travel on the Sabbath and how certain rituals were to be performed. Nearly seven hundred of these ritualistic laws were in effect at the time of Jesus.

2. *Asceticism,* which often took the form of self-denial. Much value was seen to be derived from fasting and withdrawing from the world so that one's senses could be sharpened and one's appreciation for the "finer things in life" could be refined. The Greeks regarded beauty as a very high ideal.

3. *Mysticism,* which was a concern for all things that were ethereal and unknown. For example, pagan Greeks often sought information from "oracles," who usually functioned in a drug-induced trance and in a cloud of incense that was also laced with drugs.

4. *Hedonism,* which was the Greek belief that the spirit was of supreme importance and the body was simply to be "used" by man. From one perspective, the body was to be subjected into strict discipline so that the spirit of man might more effectively function and be more clearly reflected to others. From a near opposite perspective, the body could also be abused through excessive drinking, gluttony, and numerous sexual encounters because in the end, the body was of little importance.

• *In your life, can you see areas in which you may have been influenced toward one or more of these strains of thought?*

Legalism— _____

*Asceticism —*_____

Mysticism— _____

Hedonism— _____

• *What were the results?*

_____

_____

What are some of the ways these four streams of thought are manifested in our world today? Consider the following statements that are heard often but are directly opposed to the gospel:

1. Legalism. "You have to know the rules of the game if you are going to be a winner." "If you don't keep all of God's rules, God is going to judge you." "If you break too many of God's rules or break them too often, you lose your chance of being forgiven."

What does the gospel say? Jesus taught, "Unless one is born again, he cannot see the kingdom of God . . . You must be born again" (John 3:3, 7).

What the Word Says	What the Word Says to Me
By the deeds of the law no flesh will be justified in His sight . . . Man is justified by faith apart from the deeds of the law. (Rom. 3:20, 28)	_____ _____ _____ _____ _____
If you confess with your mouth the Lord Jesus and believe in	_____ _____

your heart that God has raised
Him from the dead, you will
be saved. For with the heart
one believes unto righteousness, and with the mouth
confession is made unto salvation. (Rom. 10:9–10)

- *In what ways are you feeling challenged in your spirit?*

2. *Asceticism.* "I have to work out two hours a day and keep
my body in tip-top shape if I'm going to succeed in this life."
"The clothes make the man." "Being beautiful is more important than being smart." "Success is the best revenge."
What does the gospel say? Jesus taught,

"Blessed are the poor in spirit,
For theirs is the kingdom of heaven.
Blessed are those who mourn,
For they shall be comforted.
Blessed are the meek,
For they shall inherit the earth,
Blessed are those who hunger and thirst for
righteousness,
For they shall be filled." (Matt. 5:3–6)

What the Word Says	What the Word Says to Me
[Jesus said,] "Do not lay up for yourselves treasures on earth, where moth and rust destroy and where thieves break in and steal; but lay up for yourselves	

treasures in heaven, where neither moth nor rust destroys
and where thieves do not break
in and steal." (Matt. 6:19–20)

[Jesus taught,] "Do not worry
about your life, what you will
eat or what you will drink; nor
about your body, what you will
put on. Is not life more than
food and the body more than
clothing?" (Matt. 6:25)

Bodily exercise profits a little,
but godliness is profitable for
all things, having promise of
the life that now is and of that
which is to come. (1 Tim. 4:8)

[Jesus said,] "If anyone desires
to come after Me, let him deny
himself, and take up his cross,
and follow Me. For whoever
desires to save his life will lose
it, but whoever loses his life for
My sake will find it. For what
profit is it to a man if he gains
the whole world, and loses his
own soul? Or what will a man
give in exchange for his soul?"
(Matt. 16:24–26)

- *In what ways are you feeling challenged in your spirit?*

3. Mysticism. "It's not wrong to dabble in various New Age practices because these things can make me more spiritual." "All religions are equal so it's good to try various ones to see which ones work for you."

What does the gospel say? "Jesus said to him, 'I am the way, the truth, and the life. No one comes to the Father except through Me'" (John 14:6).

What the Word Says	What the Word Says to Me
[Jesus said,] "I am the light of the world. He who follows Me shall not walk in darkness, but have the light of life." (John 8:12)	_____
Beloved, do not believe every spirit, but test the spirits, whether they are of God; because many false prophets have gone out into the world. By this you know the Spirit of God: Every spirit that confesses that Jesus Christ has come in the flesh is of God, and every spirit that does not confess that Jesus Christ has come in the flesh is not of God. (1 John 4:1–3)	_____

- *In what ways are you feeling challenged in your spirit?*

_____

_____

4. Hedonism. "If it feels good, do it." "Try it, you might like it." "Eat, drink, and be merry." "If you can't afford it, charge it."

What does the gospel say? Jesus taught, "Let your light so shine before men, that they may see your good works and glorify your Father in heaven" (Matt. 5:16). We are not to live for our own pleasure, but rather, to give pleasure to God through loving service and a pure witness to others.

What the Word Says	What the Word Says to Me
By faith Moses, when he became of age, refused to be called the son of Pharaoh's daughter, choosing rather to suffer affliction with the people of God than to enjoy the passing pleasures of sin, esteeming the reproach of Christ greater riches than the treasures in Egypt; for he looked to the reward. (Heb. 11:24–26)	
[Jesus said,] "Enter by the narrow gate; for wide is the gate and broad is the way that leads to destruction, and there are many who go in by it. Because narrow is the gate and difficult is the way which leads to life, and there are few who find it." (Matt. 7:13–14)	
Then Jesus, looking at him, loved him, and said to him, "One thing you lack: Go your way, sell whatever you have and give to the poor, and you	

will have treasure in heaven; and come, take up the cross, and follow Me." But he was sad at this word, and went away sorrowful, for he had great possessions. (Mark 10:21–22)

- *In what ways are you feeling challenged today?*

_____

_____

- *How do you feel about taking a stand for the gospel and against the philosophy of the world?*

_____

_____

Turning Away from the "Principles of the World"

What are the principles of the world? Four of the main principles by which the world systems operate are these:

1. *Man is sufficient unto himself.* In other words, man is an end unto himself. The world proclaims that man has the ability to decide within himself what to think and how to act, and that no redemption of man is necessary since man can determine his own fate through acts of his will alone.

2. *Today is all that matters.* The world is very "now" focused—we live in a society that demands instant gratification and immediate rewards. While Jesus certainly taught us to live in the present moment, trusting God for every hour of our lives, He also taught that we are to recognize that our faith and our actions have eternal consequences.

3. *Happiness can be bought.* It can be generated by the possession

or use of things, including alcohol, drugs, and other substances taken into the body.

4. "Fate" determines many things in life. Stress, for example, is blamed for causing many things when in many cases, misplaced priorities and sin—both of which are subject to human will and human choices—are at the root of the problem. To believe in fate is to deny the omnipotence and omniscience of God. It is to say that there are moments in one's life in which God is not involved, does not know what is happening, or is not in control. Many people turn to astrology and horoscopes believing that they can find a clue there as to what will lie ahead for them on any given day; the Bible calls such practices idolatry because they put one's reliance on "fate" rather than on trust in God.

- *In your life, have you ever felt yourself giving in to these four "principles of the world"?*

_____

_____

Many Christians find themselves victims to these worldly principles. Some live as if the weight of the world has fallen on their shoulders. They are burdened and frustrated by all the responsibilities they have—they vacillate between the aspirin bottle and antacid tablets to relieve their headaches and their upset stomachs. Other Christians look for their faith to pay instant rewards—if they don't receive from God what they desire immediately, they begin to doubt God or turn away from God. Still others look to external things to generate their happiness or to dictate what happens to them in a day.

Again, Paul's response to these worldly principles would be: Don't be cheated! Don't be taken captive! Instead, take the full truth of God's Word into your mind and live by it day by day, regardless of circumstances and temporary setbacks. Read what the gospel says below.

What the Word Says	What the Word Says to Me
[Jesus said,] "Therefore I say to you, do not worry about your life, what you will eat or what you will drink; nor about your body, what you will put on. Is not life more than food and the body more than clothing? Look at the birds of the air, for they neither sow nor reap nor gather into barns; yet your heavenly Father feeds them. Are you not of more value than they? Which of you by worrying can add one cubit to his stature?" (Matt. 6:25–27)	_____
[Jesus said,] "Seek first the kingdom of God and His righteousness, and all these things shall be added to you." (Matt. 6:33)	_____
[Jesus said,] "Lay up for yourselves treasures in heaven, where neither moth nor rust destroys and where thieves do not break in and steal. For where your treasure is, there your heart will be also." (Matt. 6:20–21)	_____

Key Questions We Must Ask Ourselves

You may need to know certain facts, formulas, principles, or procedures as you make your way through this material world, but the only opinions and truth that you need for your eternal soul—both now and forever—are to be found in God's Word.

"Are you saying that the only book I should be reading is the Bible?" you might ask.

No . . . what I am saying is that when it comes to *truth* that you stake your life on, when it comes to what you *believe*, when it comes to *the foundation for your faith*, when it comes to where you turn for *meaning* that is deep, abiding, and eternal, you must turn to God's Word! No substitute will do. And furthermore, nothing *other than* the Word of God is required. Jesus Christ in you—and as His words abide in you—is your total Sufficiency for truth, meaning, and value in life. What He says is all that counts when it comes to your being born again, your relationship with God, and your eternal destiny.

There are three things you must ask of your own thinking and believing, as well as about any opinion you encounter or any philosophy that may be taught to you:

1. What am I believing that does *not* line up with the Word of God?
2. What habits do I have that do *not* line up with the Word of God?
3. Is this teaching or opinion of God or is it of man? Does it line up with the truth of God's Word?

   • *What new insights do you have into the sufficiency of Christ to give your life meaning?*

   _____

   _____

• *In what ways are you being challenged in your spirit today?*

_____

_____

ALL WE NEED FOR A VIBRANT LIFE IN THE CHURCH

As a pastor, I have come to recognize these categories of people who attend a church: those who are *active* in the life of the church; those who sit on the periphery and for the most part are *passive*—they may attend church and occasionally put something in the offering plate, but they leave the minute the service is over and are not involved in church activities or outreach; and those who drift away over time and are *inactive*—they may attend church on Christmas Eve and Easter Sunday but for the most part, they never enter the door of a church.

Why do people become passive or inactive when it comes to their life in the church? I believe the two main reasons are these: 1) They get entangled in sin of some type and they don't want to confess or repent of that sin; and 2) they don't really understand what they joined when they became a church member. Many people join churches thinking they have aligned themselves with some type of religious organization, which might give them greater social status or good business contacts. If that is their motivation, they can readily become disillusioned with various church members or practices, lose interest, or move on to another organization that they hope will meet their needs for belonging and worthiness.

The apostle Paul addressed the issue of the church in his letter to the Colossians, stating about Christ Jesus,

> He is the head of the body, the church, who is the beginning, the firstborn from the dead, that in all things He may have the preeminence. (Col. 1:18)

What does it truly mean for Jesus Christ to be the head of the church? That is the focus for this lesson.

• *How do you feel about your own church membership?*

_____

_____

Christ Jesus Is the Head of the Church

The Greek term for church literally means "called out of"— the first-century Christians perceived that they had been called out of the world and set apart for God's purposes. They saw themselves as a "body" of believers under the leadership, or "headship" of Jesus Christ. The word for "church" is used in three distinct ways in the New Testament:

1. *The body of all believers*—all saved people—of all ages. A person becomes a part of this body through belief in the blood of Jesus Christ as the atonement necessary to bring about reconciliation with God and to experience forgiveness from sin by God's grace. The universal body of believers includes all people who declare Jesus Christ to be Savior and Lord.
2. *Believers in a specific locality, place, or city.* The Colossians were the believers in the city of Colosse. In writing to these believers, Paul said that his letter should be "read

also in the church of the Laodiceans" (Col. 4:16). Laodicea was a city and one or more groups of believers lived in that city.

3. *Believers in one specific group of people who met together to worship God.* In writing to the Colossians, Paul said: "Greet the brethren who are in Laodicea, and Nymphas and the church that is in his house" (Col. 4:15). The group at Nymphas's house was a "local" church.

The most prevalent meaning for the term *church* is the first—the universal body of all believers. The church is not a building or a denomination. It is *all* Christians *everywhere.* When a person believes in Jesus Christ as his or her Savior and seeks to identify with and follow Jesus Christ as Lord, that person is automatically a part of the universal church, regardless of other affiliations he or she may have.

> • *In your life, have you had experiences in local, area-wide, and the "universal" church . . . based solely on your belief in Jesus Christ apart from any type of organizational membership?*

_____

_____

Jesus Christ is the founder of the church; He is its *only* founder. In Matthew 16, Jesus asked His disciples what others were saying about Him. He then asked the disciples directly, "But who do you say that I am?" Simon Peter answered and said, "You are the Christ, the Son of the living God."

Jesus responded to Peter this way:

Blessed are you, Simon Bar-Jonah, for flesh and blood has not revealed this to you, but My Father who is in heaven. And I also say to you that you are Peter, and on this rock I will build My church, and the gates of Hades shall not prevail against it. (Matt. 16:17–18)

On the basis of this passage of Scripture, there are those who say that Peter was the founder of the church. Jesus, however, was not building the church on *Peter*, but rather on the truth of the statement that Peter made: Jesus is the Christ, the Son of the living God. It is those who believe this truth who are genuine *church* members.

- *What new insights do you have into this passage from Matthew 16?*

Why is it so important for us to recognize what the church is and who the founder of the church is? Because Jesus Christ is both the way a person enters the church and He is the One who causes the church to exist, to function, to prosper and grow, and to be used to extend His kingdom on this earth. You can have a social club, an organization, and even a religious group without Jesus Christ . . . but you cannot have a genuine church without Jesus Christ as its founder, head, and ongoing source of spiritual life. You can meet with a group of people to follow a ritual or sing songs or hear lectures . . . but you cannot truly function as a church unless Jesus Christ is central to all that you do. He is the Sufficiency for the church; indeed, He alone is the Creator and the Sustainer of His church.

The church is a living *organism*, not an organization. It is alive and spiritual. It is the *body* of Christ.

What the Word Says	What the Word Says to Me
For as the body is one and has many members, but all the members of that one body,	_____ _____ _____

being many, are one body, so
also is Christ. For by one
Spirit we were all baptized into
one body—whether Jews or
Greeks, whether slaves or
free—and have all been made
to drink into one Spirit.
(1 Cor. 12:12–13)

Now you are the body of
Christ, and members individually. (1 Cor. 12:27)

So continuing daily with one
accord in the temple, and
breaking bread from house to
house, they ate their food with
gladness and simplicity of
heart, praising God and having
favor with all the people. And
the Lord added to the church
daily those who were being
saved. (Acts 2:46–47)

Errors We Make About the Church

We make a grave mistake any time we think the church is:

- *Limited to a particular denomination.* Denominations were
  never God's intention or design. Denominations formed
  on the basis of doctrine (beliefs) and polity (organization).
  They often reflect different approaches to styles of worship and different cultural backgrounds. The church as a
  whole includes people from many denominations who
  truly believe that Jesus is the Christ.

- *Any religious group that calls itself a church.* A number of cults exist today that deny the deity of Christ Jesus and yet still claim to be a "church." The plain and simple fact is that if Jesus Christ is not regarded as the Son of God and if He isn't the head, the "body" isn't a church!
- *Something that we can join apart from an active faith in Jesus Christ and a reliance upon Him as our Savior.* Signing the membership roll of a church does not make a person a Christian. Baptism as an infant does not result in the conversion of the human heart. Going through various church rituals "by rote" because a person reaches a particular age or finishes a particular class does not make a person a member of the body of Christ. Only those who, with their wills, accept Jesus Christ as the substitutionary, definitive, and only necessary sacrifice for their sin, and who believe in Jesus Christ as Savior can be members of the church.

What the Word Says

For you are all sons of God through faith in Christ Jesus. For as many of you as were baptized into Christ have put on Christ. There is neither Jew nor Greek, there is neither slave nor free, there is neither male nor female; for you are all one in Christ Jesus. (Gal. 3:26–28)

There is one body and one Spirit, just as you were called in one hope of your calling; one Lord, one faith, one baptism; one God and Father

What the Word Says to Me

_____

_____

_____

_____

_____

_____

_____

_____

_____

_____

_____

_____

_____

of all, who is above all, and
through all, and in you all.
(Eph. 4:4–6)

For we, though many, are one
bread and one body; for we all
partake of that one bread.
(1 Cor. 10:17)

- *In what ways are you feeling challenged in your spirit today?*

A Matter of "Dead or Alive"

The real issue associated with your being a part of the church—Christ's own body—is not whether you are an active member, a passive member, or an inactive member. It is much more serious than that. Membership in an organization may have degrees of activity. Being part of an organism is something else entirely. It is a matter of *life and death spiritually*.

When one part of a body dies, it often turns gangrenous and the result will be death unless that dead tissue is removed. When one part of a body dies, the entire body suffers.

This is also true in the church. Jesus Christ *is* the life of the church. It is His life that flows into each member of the church, great or small. It is His life that gives life, vibrancy, purpose, meaning, fulfillment, and energy to each member and to the whole. Paul wrote this very plainly to the Colossians: "When Christ *who is our life* appears, then you also will appear with Him in glory" (Col. 3:4, emphasis added).

Christ who is our life! Without Him, you are spiritually dead. With Him, you are alive. The question to ask always, however, is this: *How* alive am I?

We each know the difference between having just enough

energy to get out of bed and go through the motions of a day, and having abundant energy that truly leads to a vitality of life and great joy, accomplishment, and effectiveness. Is your spirit vibrantly alive today? Or just barely alive?

When you accepted Jesus Christ as your Savior, you became a part of His living body. You became a branch in the living vine of Christ (see John 15:1–8). The eternal life source of the Holy Spirit began to course through every facet of your being—spirit, mind, emotions, and body.

If a person chooses to withdraw from Christ, to pursue sin, or in any way seeks to diminish the work of the Holy Spirit in his life, he slows down the pumping of the life source of the Holy Spirit into his life and through his life to others. He "clogs the vessel" of his own life. He becomes less effective, less energized by the Spirit, less healthy and whole spiritually, emotionally, and relationally. His inner self begins to atrophy, just as a muscle withers and becomes ineffective if the flow of energy through the nervous system and the blood vessels is constricted or limited.

The Lord gave a very sharp warning to the Laodicean church about the state of their spiritual life:

> I know your works, that you are neither cold nor hot. I could wish you were cold or hot. So then, because you are lukewarm, and neither cold nor hot, I will vomit you out of My mouth. Because you say, "I am rich, have become wealthy, and have need of nothing"—and do not know that you are wretched, miserable, poor, blind, and naked . . . As many as I love, I rebuke and chasten. Therefore be zealous and repent. (Rev. 3:15–17, 19)

- *What new insights do you have into this passage of Scripture?*

_____

_____

• *In what ways are you feeling challenged in your spirit?*

_____

_____

What the Word Says	What the Word Says to Me
[Jesus said,] "I am the way, the truth, and the life." (John 14:6)	_____ _____
God composed the body . . . that there should be no schism in the body, but that the members should have the same care for one another. And if one member suffers, all the members suffer with it; or if one member is honored, all the members rejoice with it. (1 Cor. 12:24–26)	_____ _____ _____ _____ _____ _____ _____ _____ _____ _____
[Jesus said,] "I have come that they may have life, and that they may have it more abundantly." (John 10:10)	_____ _____ _____ _____
His divine power has given to us all things that pertain to life and godliness. (2 Peter 1:3)	_____ _____ _____
[Jesus said,] "Without Me you can do nothing." (John 15:5)	_____ _____

He Is the One Who Makes
Our Ministry Effective

What does it mean for us to rely on Christ Jesus for our spiritual life and vibrancy—both individually and as a group of believers?

1. It means we rely totally on Jesus Christ to direct us into the ministry avenues that He wants us to pursue. Paul wrote,

> For we are God's fellow workers; you are God's field, you are God's building. According to the grace of God which was given to me, as a wise master builder I have laid the foundation, and another builds on it . . . If anyone's work which he has built on it endures, he will receive a reward. (1 Cor. 3:9–10, 14)

Ask yourself continually:

- Am I ministering to others in the way that Jesus Christ desires for me to minister?
- Am I involved in the ministry projects that the Lord desires for me to do? Or, am I doing various things for my personal glorification or simply because I didn't have the courage to say no?
- Am I listening continually for the Lord's direction so that I will be flexible and quick to act as He leads and guides me?

- *What new insights do you have into the preceding passage from 1 Corinthians?*

  _____

  _____

- *In what ways are you feeling challenged in your spirit?*

  _____

  _____

2. It means that we rely totally on Jesus Christ to make us effective. We each must do our part—using our gifts and our talents fully—but in the end, we must trust Jesus Christ to do what none of us can do. Only He can save souls, deliver from evil, and make people whole. Paul wrote clearly to the Corinthians,

> Who then is Paul, and who is Apollos, but ministers through whom you believed, as the Lord gave to each one? I planted, Apollos watered, but God gave the increase. So then neither he who plants is anything, nor he who waters, but God who gives the increase. Now he who plants and he who waters are one, and each one will receive his own reward according to his own labor. (1 Cor. 3:5–8)

Are you truly trusting God to work through you to others? Never discount what you do in the name of Jesus. Do not be reluctant to serve others because you think you can do so little or know so little. Give to Jesus what you *do* have and watch Him multiply it and use it to bless others. After all, He multiplied a little boy's lunch of five loaves and two fish (see Mark 6:37–44). What might the Lord do with what *you* give to Him!

- *In what ways are you feeling challenged in your spirit today?*

  _____

  _____

- *What new insights do you have into the sufficiency of Christ?*

  _____

  _____

ACCESSING THE SUFFICIENCY OF CHRIST JESUS

How do we access the sufficiency of Christ Jesus? How do we "tap into" His effectiveness and the richness of His character? How do we become saved, victorious, confident Christians who trust Him completely and live in His sufficiency?

The process is threefold:

1. We must *commit* ourselves to seeking the truth of God, which includes the truth of Jesus Christ's sufficiency to meet all of our needs. We must desire to know the truth of God's Word and to apply His truth to our lives.
2. We must *confess* the truth of God, and especially confess that the truth of God pertains to our personal lives.
3. We must *claim* the truth of God for our lives by our faith.

Commit to the Truth

The psalmist made a tremendous statement about the truth we find in God's Word:

> The law of the LORD is perfect, converting the soul;
> The testimony of the LORD is sure, making wise the
> simple;
> The statutes of the LORD are right, rejoicing the heart;
> The commandment of the LORD is pure, enlightening
> the eyes;
> The fear of the LORD is clean, enduring forever;
> The judgments of the LORD are true and righteous
> altogether.
> More to be desired are they than gold,
> Yea, than much fine gold;
> Sweeter also than honey and the honeycomb.
> Moreover by them Your servant is warned.
> And in keeping them there is great reward.
> (Ps. 19:7–11)

The truth does not come to us automatically. We must search it out. We must be diligent in our reading and study of God's Word so that we truly know God's opinion, God's desires, God's commandments. We must *pursue* the truth. And when we find it and follow it, we find that we experience great blessing!

- *How do you feel about the importance of pursuing the truth for every aspect of your life?*

_____

_____

What the Word Says

[Jesus said,] "If you abide in My word, you are My disciples indeed. And you shall know the truth, and the truth shall make you free." (John 8:31–32)

What the Word Says to Me

_____

_____

_____

_____

_____

_____

Buy the truth, and do not sell it,
Also wisdom and instruction and understanding. (Prov. 23:23)

And we know that the Son of God has come and has given us an understanding, that we may know Him who is true; and we are in Him who is true, in His Son Jesus Christ. This is the true God and eternal life. (1 John 5:20)

[Jesus said,] "Ask, and it will be given to you; seek, and you will find; knock, and it will be opened to you." (Matt. 7:7)

Walk as children of light (for the fruit of the Spirit is in all goodness, righteousness, and truth), finding out what is acceptable to the Lord. (Eph. 5:8–10)

- *In what ways are you feeling challenged in your spirit?*

Confess the Truth

Tremendous power is released when we confess the truth of God to ourselves and to others. To confess is to openly and directly state something. Repeatedly through the Scriptures we find that the visible world was created by the invisible word of God. Read the passage of Genesis 1 below. Note each time you find the phrase "God said."

Then God said, "Let there be light"; and there was light. And God saw the light, that it was good; and God divided the light from the darkness. God called the light Day, and the darkness He called Night. So the evening and the morning were the first day.

Then God said, "Let there be a firmament in the midst of the waters, and let it divide the waters from the waters." Thus God made the firmament, and divided the waters which were under the firmament from the waters which were above the firmament; and it was so. And God called the firmament Heaven. So the evening and the morning were the second day.

Then God said, "Let the waters under the heavens be gathered together into one place, and let the dry land appear"; and it was so. And God called the dry land Earth, and the gathering together of the waters He called Seas. And God saw that it was good. Then God said, "Let the earth bring forth grass, the herb that yields seed, and the fruit tree that yields fruit according to its kind, whose seed is in itself, on the earth"; and it was so. And the earth brought forth grass, the herb that yields seed according to its kind, and the tree that yields fruit, whose seed is in itself according to its kind. And God saw that it was good. So the evening and morning were the third day.

Then God said, "Let there be lights in the firmament of the heavens to divide the day from the night; and let them be for signs and seasons, and for days and years; and let them be for lights in the firmament of the heavens to give light on the earth"; and it was so. Then God made two great lights: the greater light to rule the day, and the lesser light to rule the night. He made the stars also. God set them in the firmament of the heavens to give light on the earth, and to rule over the day and over the night, and to divide the light from the darkness. And God saw that it was good. So the evening and the morning were the fourth day.

Then God said, "Let the waters abound with an abundance of living creatures, and let birds fly above the earth across the face of the firmament of the heavens." So God created great sea creatures and every living thing that moves, with which the waters abounded, according to their kind, and every winged bird according to its kind. And God saw that it was good. And God blessed them, saying, "Be fruitful and multiply, and fill the waters in the seas, and let birds multiply on the earth." So the evening and the morning were the fifth day.

Then God said, "Let the earth bring forth the living creature according to its kind: cattle and creeping thing and beast of the earth, each according to its kind"; and it was so. And God made the beast of the earth according to its kind, cattle according to its kind, and everything that creeps on the earth according to its kind. And God saw that it was good.

Then God said, "Let Us make man in Our image, according to Our likeness; let them have dominion over the fish of the sea, over the birds of the air, and over the cattle, over all the earth and over every creeping thing that creeps on the earth." So God created man in His own image; in the image of God He created him; male and female He created them. Then God blessed them, and God said to them, "Be fruitful and multiply; fill the earth and subdue it; have dominion over the fish of the sea, over the birds of the air, and over every living thing that moves on the earth."

And God said, "See, I have given you every herb that yields seed which is on the face of all the earth, and every tree whose fruit yields seed; to you it shall be for food. Also, to every beast of the earth, to every bird of the air, and to everything that creeps on the earth, in which there is life, I have given every green herb for food"; and it was so. Then God saw everything that He had made, and indeed it was very good. So the evening and the morning were the sixth day (Gen. 1:3–31).

God created, again and again, by speaking various aspects of our universe into existence. Then God "defined" what He had created, again by speaking His word. Read Genesis 1 again. This time note how many times you find the phrase "God called." In naming things, God was giving them an identity, a purpose, and a definition—He was expressing the "truth" of His creation and how it was to function. Also note the various ways in which God gave order and limitations to the world He made.

And finally, God established and blessed what He had made, sealing the truth of His creation through His spoken word. Read Genesis 1 yet a third time. This time note how many times you find the phrase "And God saw that it was good." God was pleased with what He had made and the way in which He had made it to function, and He established it as His law forevermore. Once God made something, defined it with various laws, and established it as "good" in His sight, the thing God made was *accomplished*. It was *true*.

- *What new insights do you have into Genesis 1?*

  _____

  _____

What does this mean for us today? It means that God made you. He made me. He spoke each of us into existence long before we were conceived in our mother's womb. He "called" you—He defined you and gave you specific talents, gifts, and dreams. All your life He has continued to call you, giving you ongoing guidance, direction, relationships, and protection. God created you and God has molded you. Any work that God has done in your life is permanent—it cannot be destroyed or taken away. It is the *truth* about who you are as His beloved child and as a person who is born again and saved forever.

- *Reflect back over your life. Identify some of the permanent things that God has done in you and for you.*

_____

_____

God speaks—and in doing so, He creates the visible from the invisible. He creates a truth that is not only truth "in theory," but truth "in reality." Paul wrote to the Romans that it is God "who gives life to the dead and calls those things which do not exist as though they did" (Rom. 4:17).

This is also an especially important concept for you to believe when it comes to those things that you "lack" but are necessary for you to have full confidence and to be fully effective. Everything that Jesus Christ speaks to you *about you, about Himself,* and *about the relationship He desires to have with you* are rock-bottom truths that you can base your life upon. Jesus Christ speaks the truth to you, and when you accept His truth and believe it and then *speak it* to yourself and others, the truth of His Word *becomes* a reality in your life.

Do you need more strength or power? Ask the Lord for it. Look for passages in God's Word that speak about the strength and power of the Lord. Receive those verses into your own heart and mind, knowing that it is the Lord who lives within you! And then confess or state those verses aloud to yourself. Proclaim the truth of God's Word to your own heart and mind.

Do you need more wisdom—the solution to a problem, the answer to a nagging question? Ask the Lord for it. As you read the Bible, look for passages that speak about the all-knowing, all-wise nature of the Lord. Accept those verses as applying to your life, because it is this same omniscient Lord who lives within you by the power of His Holy Spirit. Speak those verses aloud to your own soul.

Do you need more love? Ask the Lord to reveal to you how much He loves you. As you read His Word, pay special attention to the verses that proclaim and demonstrate Jesus Christ's great love for you. Claim those verses as your very own, for it is Jesus Christ who lives within you and who loves *you* with an everlasting love. Confess—declare, speak, say—the truth of God so that it is heard by your own ears.

It is God's invisible truth—the meaning underlying the words in your Bible—that becomes a *visible* reality in our lives when we begin to believe that truth and act on it.

- *How do you feel when you hear yourself speaking the truth of God's Word and claiming that truth as applicable to your own life?*

_____

_____

- *What new insights do you have into the process and importance of confessing the Word of God as being true for yourself?*

_____

_____

What the Word Says

As the truth is in Jesus . . . be renewed in the spirit of your

What the Word Says to Me

- -

- -

mind . . . put on the new man which was created according to God, in true righteousness and holiness. Therefore, putting away lying, "Let each one of you speak truth with his neighbor." (Eph. 4:21, 23–25)

For my mouth will speak truth. (Prov. 8:7)

He who speaks truth declares righteousness,
But a false witness, deceit. (Prov. 12:17)

[Jesus said,] "Therefore whoever confesses Me before men, him I will also confess before My Father who is heaven." (Matt. 10:32)

Every tongue should confess that Jesus Christ is Lord, to the glory of God the Father. (Phil. 2:11)

Everything the Bible says about you as a beloved child of God, one called to be a joint heir with Christ Jesus, is not only true, but it is irreversible. Once you have claimed any gift, trait, or promise offered to you freely and lovingly by the Lord Jesus Christ, it cannot be taken away from you. What you receive by your faith that is part of Jesus Christ and reflects His nature and character cannot be stripped away from you. Why is this so? Because Christ lives within you and

He never leaves you. He is present with you always and all that He is by nature is made available to you when you receive Him. How can we have any lack of confidence once we are fully aware that Jesus Christ is within us, in the manifestation of the Holy Spirit, and that we have access to all that He is?

What the Word Says	What the Word Says to Me
By faith we understand that the worlds were framed by the word of God, so that the things which are seen were not made of things which are visible. (Heb. 11:3)	
If God is for us, who can be against us? He who did not spare His own Son, but delivered Him up for us all, how shall He not with Him also freely give us all things? (Rom. 8:31–32)	
And we have such trust through Christ toward God. Not that we are sufficient of ourselves to think of anything as being from ourselves, but our sufficiency is from God. (2 Cor. 3:4–5)	
I can do all things through Christ who strengthens me. (Phil. 4:13)	

• *In what ways are you feeling challenged in your spirit?*

_____

_____

Claiming Truth

Those things that are promised to us by God and that we claim by our faith are what become the reality of truth inside us. In accepting Jesus as our Savior, we make a "faith claim"— we accept with our faith and believe that what God has said about the death of Jesus on the cross is true. And it is as we believe and receive Jesus *by faith* that Jesus becomes our Savior and the Holy Spirit begins to reside within us. This same principle applies to everything that is promised by God to us. We must claim that we *receive* it into our lives *by our faith*.

Faith is the key to receiving and accepting the sufficiency of Christ Jesus for every area of our lives. When we desire the sufficiency of Christ to be made a reality in our lives in any area of lack or need that we are experiencing, we must *receive and believe* that God's Word is true for us, and that we are in possession of all that Christ offers to us.

What the Word Says	What the Word Says to Me
Commit your way to the LORD,	_____
Trust also in Him,	_____
And He shall bring it to pass.	_____
He shall bring forth your righteousness as the light,	_____
And your justice as the noonday. (Ps. 37:5–6)	_____
	_____
According to the eternal purpose which He accomplished	_____
	_____

in Christ Jesus our Lord, in
whom we have boldness and
access with confidence through
faith in Him . . . For this reason I bow my knees to the
Father of our Lord Jesus
Christ . . . that He would grant
you, according to the riches of
His glory, to be strengthened
with might through His Spirit
in the inner man, that Christ
may dwell in your hearts
through faith. (Eph. 3:11–12,
14, 16–17)

So the Lord said, "If you have
faith as a mustard seed, you
can say to this mulberry tree,
'Be pulled up by the roots and
be planted in the sea,' and it
would obey you." (Luke 17:6)

For we through the Spirit
eagerly wait for the hope of
righteousness by faith. (Gal.
5:5)

Having been justified by faith,
we have peace with God
through our Lord Jesus Christ,
through whom also we have
access by faith into this grace
in which we stand, and rejoice
in hope of the glory of God.
(Rom. 5:1–2)

A Daily Process

Committing ourselves to the pursuit of truth, confessing the truth of God as being applicable to our own lives, and claiming by our faith that we receive the truth of Christ's sufficiency for us is a threefold *ongoing process*. We cannot commit ourselves to the truth only once—it is something we must do daily, asking the Holy Spirit to lead and guide us into all truth as Jesus promised He would (see John 16:13).

Confessing the truth of God for our own lives is something that we must do daily as we read God's Word. Every portion of the Word of God is true for you and for me. It is the *way* God intends for us to think, believe, feel, respond, speak, and act.

Receiving the truth of Christ's sufficiency is also something we must do daily. We must claim that Jesus *is* the Lord over every situation in our lives and that He is our all in all, in every circumstance and in the face of every need.

When we are faithful in doing our part—committing our minds to the truth, confessing with our mouths the truth, and claiming in our hearts the truth—then the Holy Spirit does His part in our lives. He meets all of our needs through the overflowing and glorious riches of Christ Jesus.

- *What new insights do you have into the sufficiency of Christ and how to access it in your daily life?*

_____

_____

- *In what ways are you feeling challenged in your spirit?*

_____

_____

CHOOSING TO LIVE IN HIS SUFFICIENCY

As believers in Christ Jesus, we have everything we "need" to live a victorious life and to receive eternal life.

Spiritually, we have Christ Jesus within.

Morally, we have the Holy Spirit available to help us make the right choices daily and to exemplify Christ to the world.

Mentally, we have the Holy Spirit as our Teacher and Counselor—One fully capable of leading us into all truth.

Physically and materially, we have access to the full riches in glory by Christ Jesus (Phil. 4:19).

Emotionally, we have Christ Jesus as our total Sufficiency for love, relationship, wholeness, value, worthiness, and a sense of belonging.

When we say, "I need . . ." and we complete that statement with anything other than or in addition to Christ Jesus, we begin to justify our sin or develop a rationale that is based upon a lie. The truth is that we are *complete* in Christ. He has the capacity and ability to meet all of our needs.

The question is not really one of Christ's sufficiency—He is sufficient and that is an absolute truth of God—but rather, the question is whether we have made a choice to receive Christ's sufficiency into our lives. Have we made a decision with our will to know the truth, speak the truth, receive the truth, and then live by the truth that Jesus Christ is our total Sufficiency for all needs, in all circumstances, and in all aspects of life?

If you have not made that decision to allow Jesus Christ to live in you and through you *with the abundance of His sufficiency,* I invite you to make that decision today. I encourage you to pray:

> Lord Jesus, I have been prideful and arrogant. I have lived independently from You. I confess that I have sinned against You. I ask You to forgive me of my sin of unbelief and of trying to live my life my own way and according to my own limited resources. I believe Jesus Christ died on the cross for my sins. I believe that He makes available to me through the Holy Spirit all that I need for a life that is filled to overflowing with joy, purpose, meaning, and satisfaction. I here and now accept Him as my personal Savior, Lord, and God. I lay aside all my pride and the things I have depended upon, and I look solely to You to be my complete Sufficiency.

And now . . . *look* for Christ Jesus to be your Sufficiency. I believe that if you have prayed this prayer with a sincere and humble heart, His presence, power, and supply will be revealed to you. Accept what He gives, and then freely pass it on to others!